THE FRENCH AMERICANS

Polly Morrice

CHELSEA HOUSE PUBLISHERS
New York   Philadelphia

Cover Photo: This New Orleans street band performed with homemade instruments in Storyville in the late 1890s.

Editor-in-Chief: Nancy Toff
Executive Editor: Remmel T. Nunn
Managing Editor: Karyn Gullen Browne
Copy Chief: Juliann Barbato
Picture Editor: Adrian G. Allen
Art Director: Giannella Garrett
Manufacturing Manager: Gerald Levine

Staff for THE FRENCH AMERICANS
Senior Editor: Sam Tanenhaus
Copyeditors: James Guiry, Ellen Scordato
Editorial Assistant: Theodore Keyes
Picture Researcher: PAR/NYC
Designer: Noreen M. Lamb
Layout: Phillip Sobel
Production Coordinator: Joseph Romano
Cover Illustrator: Paul Biniasz
Banner Design: Hrana L. Janto

Creative Director: Harold Steinberg

3 5 7 9 8 6 4 2

Library of Congress Cataloging in Publication Data

Morrice, Polly Alison.
   The French Americans.

   (The Peoples of North America)
   Bibliography: p.
   Includes index.
   Summary: Discusses the history, culture, and religion of the French; factors encouraging their immigration; and their acceptance as an ethnic group in North America.
   1. French Americans—Juvenile literature.
[1. French Americans] I. Title. II. Series.
E184.F8M67   1988   973'.0441   87-23886
ISBN 0-87754-878-1

      0-7910-0264-0 (pbk.)

CONTENTS

THE PEOPLES OF NORTH AMERICA

CHELSEA HOUSE PUBLISHERS

A
NATION
OF
NATIONS

Daniel Patrick Moynihan

The Constitution of the United States begins: "We the People of the United States . . ." Yet, as we know, the United States is not made up of a single group of people. It is made up of many peoples. Immigrants from Europe, Asia, Africa, and Central and South America settled in North America seeking a new life filled with opportunities unavailable in their homeland. Coming from many nations, they forged one nation and made it their own. More than 100 years ago, Walt Whitman expressed this perception of America as a melting pot: "Here is not merely a nation, but a teeming Nation of nations."

Although the ingenuity and acts of courage of these immigrants, our ancestors, shaped the North American way of life, we sometimes take their contributions for granted. This fine series, *The Peoples of North America,* examines the experiences and contributions of the immigrants and how these contributions determined the future of the United States and Canada.

Immigrants did not abandon their ethnic traditions when they reached the shores of North America. Each ethnic group had its own customs and traditions, and each brought different experiences, accomplishments, skills, values, styles of dress, and tastes in food that lingered long after its arrival. Yet this profusion of differences created a singularity, or bond, among the immigrants.

The United States and Canada are unusual in this respect. Whereas religious and ethnic differences have sparked intolerance throughout the rest of the world—from the 17th-century religious wars to the 19th-century nationalist movements in Europe to the near extermination of the Jewish people under Nazi Germany— North Americans have struggled to learn how to respect each other's differences and live in harmony.

Millions of immigrants from scores of homelands brought diversity to our continent. In a mass migration, some 12 million immigrants passed through the waiting rooms of New York's Ellis Island; thousands more came to the West Coast. At first, these immigrants were welcomed because labor was needed to meet the demands of the Industrial Age. Soon, however, the new immigrants faced the prejudice of earlier immigrants who saw them as a burden on the economy. Legislation was passed to limit immigration. The Chinese Exclusion Act of 1882 was among the first laws closing the doors to the promise of America. The Japanese were also effectively excluded by this law. In 1924, Congress set immigration quotas on a country-by-country basis.

Such prejudices might have triggered war, as they did in Europe, but North Americans chose negotiation and compromise, instead. This determination to resolve differences peacefully has been the hallmark of the peoples of North America.

The remarkable ability of Americans to live together as one people was seriously threatened by the issue of slavery. It was a symptom of growing intolerance in the world. Thousands of settlers from the British Isles had arrived in the colonies as indentured servants, agreeing to work for a specified number of years on farms or as apprentices in return for passage to America and room and board. When the first Africans arrived in the then-British colonies during the 17th century, some colonists thought that they too should be treated as indentured servants. Eventually, the question of whether the Africans should be viewed as indentured, like the English, or as slaves who could be owned for life, was considered in a Maryland court. The court's calamitous decree held that blacks were slaves bound to lifelong servitude, and so were their children.

America went through a time of moral examination and civil war before it finally freed African slaves and their descendants. The principle that all people are created equal had faced its greatest challenge and survived.

Yet the court ruling that set blacks apart from other races fanned flames of discrimination that burned long after slavery was abolished—and that still flicker today. The concept of racism had existed for centuries in countries throughout the world. For instance, when the Manchus conquered China in the 13th century, they decreed that Chinese and Manchus could not intermarry. To impress their superiority on the conquered Chinese, the Manchus ordered all Chinese men to wear their hair in a long braid called a queue.

By the 19th century, some intellectuals took up the banner of racism, citing Charles Darwin. Darwin's scientific studies hypothesized that highly evolved animals were dominant over other animals. Some advocates of this theory applied it to humans, asserting that certain races were more highly evolved than others and thus were superior.

This philosophy served as the basis for a new form of discrimination, not only against nonwhite people but also against various ethnic groups. Asians faced harsh discrimination and were depicted by popular 19th-century newspaper cartoonists as depraved, degenerate, and deficient in intelligence. When the Irish flooded American cities to escape the famine in Ireland, the cartoonists caricatured the typical "Paddy" (a common term for Irish immigrants) as an apelike creature with jutting jaw and sloping forehead.

By the 20th century, racism and ethnic prejudice had given rise to virulent theories of a Northern European master race. When Adolf Hitler came to power in Germany in 1933, he popularized the notion of Aryan supremacy. "Aryan," a term referring to the Indo-European races, was applied to so-called superior physical characteristics such as blond hair, blue eyes, and delicate facial features. Anyone with darker and heavier features was considered inferior. Buttressed by these theories, the German Nazi state from

1933 to 1945 set out to destroy European Jews, along with Poles, Russians, and other groups considered inferior. It nearly succeeded. Millions of these people were exterminated.

The tragedies brought on by ethnic and racial intolerance throughout the world demonstrate the importance of North America's efforts to create a society free of prejudice and inequality.

A relatively recent example of the New World's desire to resolve ethnic friction nonviolently is the solution the Canadians found to a conflict between two ethnic groups. A long-standing dispute as to whether Canadian culture was properly English or French resurfaced in the mid-1960s, dividing the peoples of the French-speaking Quebec Province from those of the English-speaking provinces. Relations grew tense, then bitter, then violent. The Royal Commission on Bilingualism and Biculturalism was established to study the growing crisis and to propose measures to ease the tensions. As a result of the commission's recommendations, all official documents and statements from the national government's capital at Ottawa are now issued in both French and English, and bilingual education is encouraged.

The year 1980 marked a coming of age for the United States's ethnic heritage. For the first time, the U.S. Census asked people about their ethnic background. Americans chose from more than 100 groups, including French Basque, Spanish Basque, French Canadian, Afro-American, Peruvian, Armenian, Chinese, and Japanese. The ethnic group with the largest response was English (49.6 million). More than 100 million Americans claimed ancestors from the British Isles, which includes England, Ireland, Wales, and Scotland. There were almost as many Germans (49.2 million) as English. The Irish-American population (40.2 million) was third, but the next largest ethnic group, the Afro-Americans, was a distant fourth (21 million). There was a sizable group of French ancestry (13 million), as well as of Italian (12 million). Poles, Dutch, Swedes, Norwegians, and Russians followed. These groups, and other smaller ones, represent the wondrous profusion of ethnic influences in North America.

Canada, too, has learned more about the diversity of its population. Studies conducted during the French/English conflict showed that Canadians were descended from Ukrainians, Germans, Italians, Chinese, Japanese, native Indians, and Eskimos, among others. Canada found it had no ethnic majority, although nearly half of its immigrant population had come from the British Isles. Canada, like the United States, is a land of immigrants for whom mutual tolerance is a matter of reason as well as principle.

The people of North America are the descendants of one of the greatest migrations in history. And that migration is not over. Koreans, Vietnamese, Nicaraguans, Cubans, and many others are heading for the shores of North America in large numbers. This mix of cultures shapes every aspect of our lives. To understand ourselves, we must know something about our diverse ethnic ancestry. Nothing so defines the North American nations as the motto on the Great Seal of the United States: *E Pluribus Unum*—Out of Many, One. ✎

In Canada, French culture has flourished for centuries, typically in academies such as St. Augustin's Academy for Boys in Quebec, pictured here.

THE FRENCH IN AMERICA

In the winter of 1848, revolution broke out in Paris. French radicals surged into the streets, toppling the regime of Louis Philippe—France's "citizen king." Some months later and a continent away, John Marshall discovered gold in California.

These two events may seem unrelated, yet together they set the stage for a most unusual episode in the history of French immigration to the United States. Weary of riots and fighting in their streets and beset by unemployment, French citizens listened attentively to glowing reports of the tremendous fortunes prospectors were making in the goldfields of California. In 1849, as France sank into an economic depression, boats packed with gold seekers sailed from the ports of Bordeaux, Marseille, and Le Havre, bound for San Francisco.

"Everyone has rushed here," a French journalist wrote, "merchants, workmen, clerks, women, old men, children, everyone, from the peasant to the man of the world." The flood of French humanity that flowed through the Golden Gate included cooks, hairdressers, doctors, and architects, as well as adventurers, petty criminals, and impoverished noblemen who hoped to restore their ruined fortunes. In just a few years, nearly 30,000 French poured into California, two-thirds of them in 1851 alone.

Of course, the French represented only a small segment of the multitude lured by the promise of easy riches. People from all over the world raced to San Francisco after hearing of Marshall's discovery. Like these other "49ers," those from France felt their lust for gold dim after their discovery that the streets of San Francisco did not glitter with the precious stuff.

But something else set the Gallic miners apart from their fellow prospectors: The sudden influx of French gold seekers in America constituted the greatest single French migration to the New World and broke a 300–year-old pattern of slow, steady migration in small groups.

French Immigration

The story of France's presence in America starts in the 16th century, shortly after the European discovery of North America, when French explorers laid claim to Canada, the Great Lakes region, and all the territory drained by the Mississippi River, from the Appalachian mountain range in the east to the Rockies in the west. A few colonists, fur traders, and missionaries followed, giving France an uneasy foothold in these vast lands. In 1763, after a series of wars with Britain, France lost most of its North American possessions. Although it still housed approximately 75,000 French-speaking people, the land that had been christened New France now belonged to Britain and Spain.

About 60,000 of the French colonists lived in areas now encompassed by Canada. Their French-speaking descendants—a total of more than 6 million—still compose a close-knit community concentrated in the eastern provinces of Quebec, Nova Scotia, and New Brunswick. Farther south, in territory that has since been added to the United States, the early French population numbered about 15,000. The majority clustered in Louisiana, where French influence continues to flavor New Orleans.

In the late 17th and early 18th centuries, the first group of French immigrants were joined by a second when thousands of Huguenots—Protestants fleeing from religious persecution in France—crossed the Atlantic, settling throughout the 13 British colonies. English speakers translated or simply mangled French Huguenot names: Feuillevert became Greenleaf; Bouquet changed to Buckett. Most Huguenot immigrants prospered as artisans, plantation owners, or political leaders. Their descendants now inhabit every region of the United States.

Throughout the 18th century and into the 19th, French migration continued. Political upheavals in France forced hosts of refugees to leave their homeland; after the Revolution of 1789 nobles, who feared losing their wealth or their lives under the new republican order, decamped to the United States. In 1815, when the French monarchy was restored, supporters of the fallen emperor Napoleon Bonaparte made their way overseas. Merchants, musicians, dancing masters, and restaurant owners also migrated to the cities of America's East Coast, setting up shops that catered to the increasingly sophisticated tastes of the young country.

In about 1820, the era of mass European migration to America began. Some French joined this transatlantic movement, drawn by reports of boundless opportunity, but French immigration in the 19th and 20th centuries never equaled that from other European countries. According to figures compiled by the United States Immigration and Naturalization Service, immigration from France during the years 1820 through

In the 17th and 18th centuries, French Protestants—or Huguenots—fled the oppression of their Catholic homeland.

Sumptuous French habits are spiritedly depicted in this late-18th-century engraving.

1984 totaled 764,000. By contrast, more than 7 million Germans emigrated to the United States in the same period; Italian, Irish, Scandinavian, and other newcomers also numbered in the millions.

Why did so few French come to the United States? One reason cited by a 19th-century scholar was the typical French person's "attachment to his native soil"— an attachment that included a love for the French language and culture. Secondly, French citizens who wished to emigrate during the 19th century were more likely to respond to official encouragement to colonize the possessions of the French empire, such as French Algeria, rather than settle in entirely alien lands. A third factor, and perhaps the most important, was France's stable population growth.

Between 1850 and 1940, the French population grew only by about 10 percent, from 36 million to 40 million people. Endowed with general prosperity and low population density, France itself attracted immigrants from other parts of Europe. Indeed, up until World War II, France received more immigrants than any other country except the United States—and without these millions of new residents, the French population would actually have decreased.

After the middle of the 19th century, the French had no compelling reason to emigrate. Those who broke with custom and left their country seemed to have in common an individualistic character. In *Intellect and Pride: France 1848–1945*, Theodore Zeldin comments that

> the people who went out from France were in general
> not driven out by poverty or unemployment; many
> of them were . . . individuals, making their own choice,
> rather than participating in a mass movement; they
> were often artisans or even professional men anxious to
> make a fortune and to use their skills in a new
> environment.

No terrible famine, like the one Ireland suffered in the 1840s, starved French artisans and professionals out of their ancestral land. Unlike many immigrants, who shipped out in a desperate attempt to improve their lot, French immigrants often came from the middle class and possessed skills and funds to ease their way. They knew that if the New World proved unsatisfying, they could always go home again.

French Canadian Immigration

Despite the small immigration from France, the French established a significant presence in the United States via Canada. Starting in the 18th century, French settlers in Canada moved south, bringing along customs and a language modified by several generations of life in North America.

Some French-Canadian immigrants were farmers and fishers from the former French province of Acadia. Driven into exile by the British government, forcibly shipped from their Nova Scotia home to the 13 colonies and even back to France, they endured many hardships. Several thousand Acadians settled in the bayous, prairies, and marshlands of southwest Louisiana, where they gradually became known as "Cajuns" (from *'ca-dien*, the French contraction for Acadian). Living in rural isolation, the Cajuns developed a distinctive French-speaking culture. Today, close to a million of their descendants still live in Louisiana and east Texas. Proud of their heritage, they seek to preserve their way of life.

In the late 1830s other French Canadians started streaming into the United States from the province of Quebec. Although most had farmed for a living back home, the majority settled in urban New England and went to work—often as young children—in the textile mills. These French Canadians preserved their culture by speaking French and living and marrying among themselves. Today, many of their approximately 1.5 million descendants still reside in New England and work in all professions. Like the Cajuns, these Franco-Americans have taken new interest in their ethnic roots.

Immigrant Individuals

From the first adventurers who settled New France to 20th-century expatriates such as artist Marcel Duchamp (a refugee from Nazi-occupied France who elected to stay on in the United States), the French have come to America for many different reasons. Explorers, political and religious exiles, fortune seekers, and others have found their way to these shores. Taken together, the descendants of all these individuals form a significant group. In 1980, census figures showed that the United States had 14 million residents of French descent. Three million of them reported that both their parents had French blood; the remainder trace mixed backgrounds that include French ancestry.

Of these 14 million people, probably few are descended from the French gold seekers who arrived during the rush of 1849. Most prospectors stayed in California only briefly before drifting to Mexico to try their luck mining or returning to France. Yet when the

wave of French 49ers receded from California, it left its mark on the local geography in the form of place-names such as French Bay and Les Fourcades.

A closer look at the map of the 50 states confirms that French place-names appear everywhere in the United States, dotting prairies and mountain ranges and cropping up along the banks of the Mississippi River in La Crosse, St. Louis, Cape Girardeau, Baton Rouge, and New Orleans. But these are not the legacy of the French gold seekers. Instead, they serve as tangible reminders of the early French settlements in America—settlements whose story properly begins several centuries ago, in France. ∾

A cartoon satirizes the great variety of European prospectors who rushed to the "gold hills" of California in 1849.

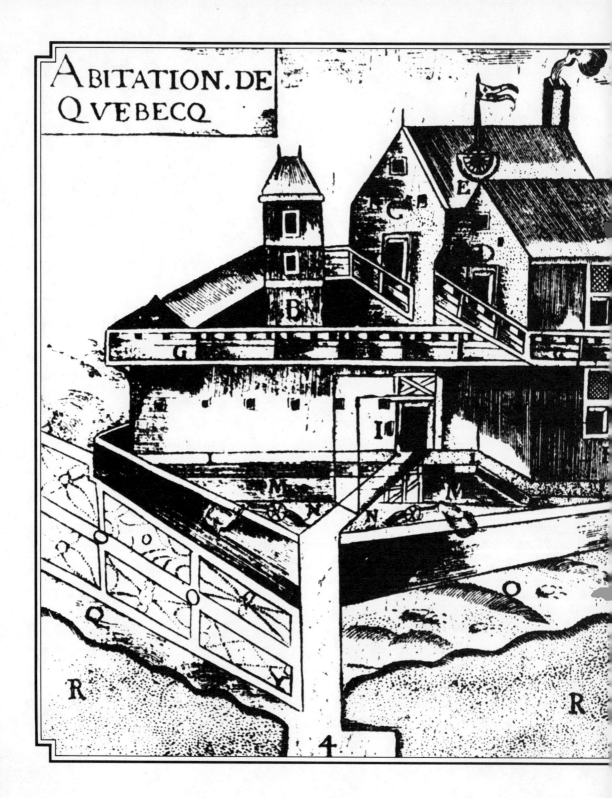

The habitation—*or colony*—*of Quebec was established in the early 17th century.*

FRANCE ON THE MAP

The first French king to turn his gaze toward the New World was the handsome 16th-century monarch Francis I, who reigned during the Renaissance, a period when science and art flourished in Europe. In many ways typical of Renaissance rulers—at once splendid and unscrupulous—Francis supported the leading artists and scholars of his day but never allowed his love of knowledge to interfere with his worldly desire for power and wealth. By 1515, when he ascended the French throne, Spain and Portugal had already divided between them the charted territory of the New World. Spain, France's bitter enemy, had started filling its coffers with gold plundered from the Indian empires of Central and South America. Eager to claim a share of New World riches and to keep France from falling behind in its rivalry with Spain, Francis helped sponsor the voyage of an Italian sea captain named Giovanni da Verrazano.

In January 1524, Verrazano and his crew set out from the coast of Brittany in a single ship, sailing due west. By pursuing this course, Verrazano sought to discover a passage to the Orient that would serve as a trade shortcut to the Far East—China, India, and the Spice Islands. He hoped also to find gold and silver in abundance—wealth like that shipped home by the Spaniards in their galleons. But Verrazano failed on both counts:

The Renaissance monarch Francis I turned his gaze toward the New World in the 16th century.

He discovered neither great treasure nor a passage to China. Like most Europeans of the time, the explorer had underestimated the size of the vast North American continent.

The expedition need not have been in vain, however. Verrazano's search for a trade route led him to explore the east coast of the present United States, from South Carolina to Maine, all of which he claimed for France. This claim could have been France's first step toward founding a colony, yet nothing came of it. When Verrazano sailed back to France to report on his trip, whatever interest there might have been in a follow-up voyage was overridden by a national crisis: France was torn apart by war, and its ruler was held prisoner by Spain.

So began France's checkered efforts at colonizing North America. For the next 240 years, its colonies would suffer the consequences of wars, religious conflicts, and political intrigues. Although most of these events occurred in Europe, they had a serious impact across the Atlantic. In the 16th century, for example, French rulers were prevented from pursuing colonization of the New World because of ongoing hostility with Spain and because of the bloody religious struggle between French Catholics and Protestants that became more violent late in the century.

France's contest with Spain intensified in 1529, when Francis, his sights set on South America, made a brief, ruinous attempt to dislodge Portugal from Brazilian lands. When the campaign failed, Francis altered his colonial strategy and concentrated his efforts on the northern lands, to which Spain and Portugal held a weaker claim. In 1534 French explorer Jacques Cartier set off from the Brittany port town of Saint-Malo and headed northwest, toward the coasts of Newfoundland and Nova Scotia.

Commissioned and financed by Francis, Cartier made a total of three expeditions. The first two were intended to uncover mineral wealth and to locate a northwest passage to the Orient. Cartier's first voyage took him only as far as the entrance of the Gulf of St. Lawrence; on his second, he sailed down the St. Lawrence River, reaching the present-day site of Montreal. The explorer wintered in the New World, enduring months of stormy weather and frigid temperatures. Although many of his crew died, Cartier left Canada undiscouraged and made plans for a return trip. In 1542, on his third and final expedition, he tried to establish a colony at the site where the modern city of Quebec now stands. The result was disastrous. The long winter brought starvation, and because the settlers had no fresh fruits and vegetables to provide them with vitamin C, even the hardiest pioneers contracted scurvy and died. When spring at last arrived, the survivors were only too glad to sail home. Generations elapsed before France again tried colonization, but Cartier had made a beginning: His colony was the start of New France.

Even had these obstacles been removed, the first pioneers to land in New France would not have settled there permanently. They upheld a tradition, dating back to the early 16th century, of traveling to North America on a seasonal, temporary basis to fish the rich waters. Fleets from Saint-Malo and other Brittany ports reaped their harvests off the banks of Newfoundland, dried their catches ashore, and then sailed back to France. The fur traders constituted a slightly more permanent group of colonists. A new fashion, wearing beaver hats, had swept Europe, and the traders came to North America to exploit its abundant beaver supply. Although they stayed longer than the fishermen, the fur traders had no interest in settling down to till the soil or build cities.

Instead they pursued quick profits and adventure. Known as *voyageurs* and *coureurs de bois* (woods runners), the traders quickly learned how to track the deep forests and how to deal with local Indians. On this latter count, they fared better than did other European settlers. The Dutch and English, for example, who had arrived in North America in the early 17th century, seized Indian territories for farmland and, as a result,

In 1524, explorer Giovanni da Verrazano hoped to find a passage leading from the east coast of North America to China.

had to fend off retaliatory raids. The Spanish followed a brutal policy of conquering and enslaving natives. By contrast, the footloose coureurs de bois, shunning the plow and hoe, and with no wish to establish their own communities on tribal lands, enjoyed friendly relations with most tribes (except the fierce Iroquois).

No less mobile than the fur traders were French explorers, who discovered and annexed new territory far more quickly than French settlers could populate it. After Samuel Champlain meticulously mapped the Atlantic Coast between Nova Scotia and Martha's Vineyard in the 17th century, adventurers and missionaries rapidly expanded French claims. Frenchmen were the first Europeans to paddle the Great Lakes; in 1673, Louis Joliet and Père Marquette portaged and canoed their way to the river the Indians called "the Father of Waters"—the great Mississippi.

This waterway presented an irresistible temptation—to follow its strong current as far south as it

In 1681–82 Robert Cavelier de La Salle traced the Mississippi to its mouth, then proceeded west. In this engraving his expedition lands in Texas.

flowed—and in 1681–82 Robert Cavelier de La Salle made a thousand-mile journey that led him all the way to the marshy delta at the river's mouth. In triumph, he erected a column, claimed all the lands watered by the river for King Louis XIV of France, and christened the entire territory stretching from the Appalachians to the Rocky Mountains "Louisiana." The sheer size of La Salle's claim helps explain why 31 of the United States were discovered, explored, or colonized by French and French Canadians. The geographical range of their efforts was enormous. In 1743, for instance, a French Canadian named LaVérendrye became one of the first Europeans to glimpse the Rocky Mountains. His father had already discovered *la chute de la pierre jaune*—Yellowstone Falls.

At the start of the 18th century, New France had taken on the shape of a V, with its vertex at the mouth of the Mississippi and it arms extended outward to encompass land on both sides of northern Canada. The French government made numerous efforts to import colonists to settle these far-flung lands, with mixed results. In 1713, about 18,000 settlers inhabited New France, clustered mostly in Montreal and Quebec and along the stretch of the St. Lawrence River linking the two cities. A small group of French fishers, trappers, and farmers lived in the eastern province of Acadia, which had recently fallen into British hands. South of Canada, a string of French forts had sprung up along the banks of the Mississippi and at other strategic sites, including present-day Pittsburgh. These garrisons served as a line of defense against the swelling British colonies to the east. Elsewhere, La Mothe Cadillac had founded Detroit as a center for the fur trade. Not for several years would the French establish the prosperous settlement called New Orleans.

Despite all these preparations, the year 1713 was a peaceful one in New France because of a treaty signed in Europe by the two clashing powers. Even so, conditions in the colonies would not remain tranquil for long. In the 17th century, constant skirmishes between French and British colonists and their respective Indian

Fur traders were the most romantic figures in 17th- and 18th-century New France.

Native Canadians—or Indians—frequently swapped their furs for rifles from French colonists.

allies had ushered in two wars, colonial extensions of conflicts being fought on the European continent. In the next century, hostilities between France and Britain extended to the colonies both had established in the New World.

The few thousand French settlers felt pressure from the hundreds of thousands of British settlers; that pressure was intensified by the competing modes of expansion the two groups had developed. The French tended to colonize in a north-south pattern, following the course of the leading waterways. The British settlers, by contrast, had started by organizing coastal settlements—at Jamestown, Virginia, and Plymouth, Massachusetts—and then moved steadily westward. Now, land-hungry British farmers were pressing toward the Appalachians, enviously eyeing the Illinois country, which was guarded by a chain of a French forts. Further collisions seemed inevitable.

The People of New France

In the 17th and 18th centuries, New France's equivalent to a modern-day get-rich-quick scheme was the fur trade. No money or training was required to try one's hand at trapping or trading, and nearly 15,000 fur traders (the coureurs de bois) set out from Montreal, seeking backwoods fortunes. Typically outfitted in leather leggings, bead-trimmed leather shirts, and brightly colored sashes, the coureurs were perhaps the most romantic figures in New France, although their practice of plying the Indians with brandy and then inducing them to sell their furs below cost dims their allure.

French-Canadian outposts also included *habitants*, farmers who usually built houses along riverbanks, cultivating long, narrow plots of land. Another group consisted of prosperous young men who had fallen into disgrace in France and were shipped overseas to redeem themselves; these ne'er-do-wells enlivened—and sometimes scandalized—colonial society. Added to the blend were poachers, smugglers, and counterfeiters who had been expelled from France.

By the late 17th century, these various French Canadians shared traits that made them a unified and unique population, distinct from their French forebears. An aristocratic French visitor described them:

> The Canadians or Créoles are well built, sturdy, tall, strong, vigorous, enterprising, brave. . . . They are presumptuous and full of themselves, putting themselves ahead of all the nations of the earth; and unfortunately they do not have the respect that they might for their [French] relatives.

Noted for their independent spirit, French Canadians also were characterized by their deep piety, in part the result of Catholic missionaries who had been present since the first days of settlement. Members of the Recollect and Sulpician religious orders had come first, in the early 17th century. They were followed by the Jesuits—a strong-willed, dedicated order, whose attempts to convert the warlike Iroquois to Christianity often became an exercise in martyrdom. The Jesuits founded schools and hospitals, and in 1639 they helped bring to New France a group of Ursuline nuns. Skilled needlewomen, the Ursulines taught the art of embroidery to Indian girls, who in turn made it a feature of traditional tribal clothing.

Soon after their arrival, the Jesuits effectively controlled the religious life of New France. Because priests taught school and drew up legal documents, they gained much worldly influence as well. The Jesuits were strictly anti-Protestant, and in 1632 they barred French Protestants, or Huguenots, from entering the colony. Within 60 years, this rule set the course of an important migration—the flight of the Huguenots to the British colonies.

The Huguenots

In 1687, a French Huguenot named Durand de Dauphiné published an enthusiastic description of the New World region known as Virginia:

> The land is so rich and so fertile that when a man has fifty acres of ground, two menservants, a maid and some cattle, neither he nor his wife do anything but visit among their neighbors.

Durand hoped to persuade his fellow Protestants in France to settle in Virginia. At the time, the Huguenots were in dire need of refuge. Two years earlier, King Louis XIV had revoked the Edict of Nantes, which had granted a measure of civil rights to French Protestants. Forced to choose between conversion to Catholicism or flight, nearly 400,000 Huguenots opted for the latter course. Most of them made their way to England, the Netherlands, and Germany, where they were welcomed as skilled artisans in textile and other industries. A portion of this mass exodus, however, came to America.

Forbidden to enter New France, Huguenots were welcomed into British colonies. British colonial officials

In the early 17th century, Catholic nuns performed many services for the Indian population of New France.

even printed pamphlets in an effort to recruit French Protestants, and by 1700 the land that Durand had so glowingly described had drawn perhaps 1,000 Huguenots, many of whom cultivated vines for wine production. Virginia, however, was neither the first nor the main destination of the Huguenot immigrants.

As early as 1564 a group of Huguenots had founded a settlement in South Carolina. Although this tiny community was soon attacked and massacred by a Spanish naval force, Huguenot migration to North America continued. By the early 17th century, a small number of settlers had arrived; it grew substantially following the revocation of the Edict of Nantes. In all, about 15,000 Huguenots settled in the British colonies, concentrated in New York, New England, and South Carolina. The Huguenot presence was small compared to the total population, but their influence was substantial.

Huguenots brightened the somber Puritan city of Boston. Hardworking and thrifty, the Protestant newcomers became respected, prosperous merchants. In New Rochelle, New York, Huguenots taught their language to the other settlers. In the nearby city of New Paltz, Huguenots were responsible for the growing popularity of finishing schools—institutions in which girls were "finished" by means of instruction in French, needlework, and good manners, all considered proper subjects for well-bred young ladies. The Huguenots are even reputed to have improved American cooking by introducing the use of yeast and popularizing the consumption of buns, okra, artichokes, and tomatoes.

In the words of historian Howard Mumford, the French Protestants

> helped to teach the colonists how to live. Bringing them the arts, the accomplishments, the graces of the most polished civilization in the world, together with a gaiety and good humor in strong contrast to the New England or the Pennsylvania temperament, the Huguenot . . . softened the hard edges of existence.

Jesuit attempts to convert the Iroquois to Catholicism often had violent results. Here missionaries smash "heathen" idols.

Many French Protestants drifted south from the northern colonies to become planters, merchants, and local politicians. Charleston, South Carolina, became the largest and richest Huguenot center. There the French were widely admired for their charming manners and renowned for their hospitality.

Huguenot immigration ended around 1760. The group blended rather quickly into colonial British society, giving up their language and even modifying their religion. By the 1750s, most of the Huguenots' French Reformed churches had become Anglican and followed the official Church of England services. Many Huguenot descendants—among them Boston patriot Paul Revere, New York statesman John Jay, and Francis Marion, the South Carolina militia commander known as the Swamp Fox—played major roles in the Revolutionary War. By the end of the 18th century, the Huguenots who had settled in the British colonies were no longer really French; they considered themselves citizens of the new United States of America. Today, many descendants of the Huguenots live in the United States, but they are no longer a distinct, French-speaking group.

The Fall of New France

In 1763, France and Britain signed the Treaty of Paris, ending years of conflict in North America between the two great powers. France ceded to Britain all its territory east of the Mississippi, except for its island possessions in the Caribbean Sea, and so the 60,000 French living in Canada became British subjects. They continued to exist as a distinct group, but in the sparsely settled lands to the south—soon to be United States territory—the French cultural influence faded rapidly.

A few traces lingered. One 19th-century writer, commenting on the Detroit of the 1830s, recalled the parties, balls, and sleigh rides that helped the carefree French habitants pass the long winter. In 1836, a young

New France fell in 1763, but the French influence remained in cities such as Detroit, pictured here in 1794.

man writing to his relatives from the formerly French city of St. Louis boasted of "talking Parley Voo" (learning French) with the "beautiful creatures" in his French dancing school. Today the most permanent reminder of New France exists on the map of the United States, which includes nearly 5,000 French place-names. They crop up from Wisconsin to Wyoming; names such as Des Moines and Dubuque (both cities in Iowa) call up images of martyred missionaries, resourceful explorers, and bold voyageurs. Summing up their magnificence and folly, historian Francis Parkman characterized the expansion of New France as "the achievement of a gigantic ambition striving to grasp a continent. It was a vain attempt."

There is one major American city, however, where the French ambition in the New World was not spent in vain, and the French heritage remains strong and colorful. That city, founded in 1718 by an adventurous young French Canadian, is New Orleans. ∾

*New Orleans's elegant
courtyards reflect the city's
mingling of French and Spanish
culture.*

A CRESCENT CITY

F or most people, New Orleans evokes an image different from all other American cities. Its attractions are well known: jazz, Mardi Gras, and the French Quarter, with its narrow streets and ornate ironwork balconies. Founded by a French Canadian, ruled successively by France, Spain, and the United States, and spiced by influences ranging from German to Afro-Caribbean, New Orleans developed in a special way. Since the 18th century, writers and travelers have touted New Orleans as "fascinating" and "romantic" or condemned it as "sinful."

By 1718, the French had laid claim to the Louisiana territory for almost 40 years, yet they had made limited progress in establishing settlements. At the turn of the century, King Louis XIV had sent a French-Canadian naval hero, Sieur d'Iberville, to lead a colonization effort in the Mississippi country. Iberville made several voyages and established forts near present-day Mobile, Alabama, and Pensacola, Florida. He also set up a fort at a site in southern Louisiana. In April 1718, Iberville's brother, Sieur de Bienville, ordered the ground cleared for a new city to be laid out along "one of the most beautiful crescents" of the Mississippi River. New Orleans thus began as a few wooden huts on swampy delta land.

In the 18th century, the Scotsman John Law (depicted here) persuaded Louis XV that Louisiana held the key to restoring France's shaky economy.

The expansion of Louisiana and the growth of New Orleans were due to the efforts of a trading organization sponsored by the French crown. A brilliant but wayward Scot named John Law convinced King Louis XV that he could restore France's shaky finances by taking advantage of the opportunities offered by French lands in the New World. He established the Company of the West, luring subscribers into investing in Louisiana, enticing them with extravagant, glowing (but false) reports of gold and silver mines and precious stones, and promising a mild climate and easy living. These subscribers were mostly French, although several groups of Germans also set off for Louisiana. Less desirable colonists, swept from French prisons, were imported by force. When these settlers arrived, after a perilous crossing, they were shocked to find a land of tropical heat, humidity, storms, floods, and mosquitoes.

In December 1720, John Law's inflated "Mississippi Bubble" collapsed, and he fled France, leaving thousands of people ruined and the country's finances in disarray. Louisiana, however, had profited from Law's schemes: By 1721 the colony and its capital city, New Orleans, had achieved a secure footing. The population had multiplied from an initial 400 to about

8,000, including black slaves. Two French engineers, Le Blond de la Tour and Adrien de Pauger, laid out a grid around a square facing the Mississippi, which became the foundation for the picturesque *Vieux Carré*—the French Quarter.

In the beginning, New Orleans's progress was uneven. Hurricanes struck often; indeed, a major storm flattened the city in 1722. The human climate was equally volatile, as the uneasy mix of aristocrats and criminals frequently erupted in gambling and fighting. Worse, Bienville and the other French officials squabbled over political issues. Like New France, the Louisiana territory was officially Roman Catholic, yet priests were few and the church held small sway. The 19th-century New Orleans novelist George Washington Cable described the fledgling city as "*sans religion, sans justice, sans discipline, sans ordre et sans police.*" (Substitute "lacking" for "*sans,*" and Cable's meaning is clear.) Despite its many problems, though, New Orleans was slowly developing a special culture.

The French Quarter—shown here in a wood engraving from the 1850s—was characterized by modest homes and shops.

In 1727, a group of marriageable young girls arrived bearing wooden trunks stuffed with dowries of linen and household goods. Subsequently labeled *filles à cassette*, or Casket Girls, these new arrivals were placed under the care of Ursuline nuns until they wed. They rarely had to wait long—they were greatly outnumbered by prospective husbands. An Ursuline nun, Sister Marie Madeleine, described New Orleans as "very handsome, well-constructed, and regularly built" but complained of a fondness for opulence and extravagant display among New Orleans's wealthy residents:

> There is so much luxury in this town that there is no distinction among the classes so far as dress goes. . . . Most of [the women] reduce themselves and their family to a hard lot of living at home. . . . and flaunt abroad in robes of velvet and damask, ornamented with the most costly ribbons.

Later, when Spain ruled the colony, the leading French and Spanish families intermarried, and their

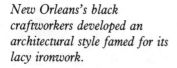

New Orleans's black craftworkers developed an architectural style famed for its lacy ironwork.

descendants carried on the tradition of *joie de vivre*. Known as *Créoles* (the term probably derives from the Spanish *criollo*, from the verb "to create"), they dressed in splendor (some tramped through the muddy, unpaved streets wearing cloth spun from gold), enjoyed frequent festivities, and filled their crudely built houses with costly furniture. In 1743, when the new colonial governor, Vaudreuil, arrived, he hosted a round of balls and banquets where tables were set with crystal and gold plate, fine wines, and sumptuous food. One of the colony's most popular governors, Vaudreuil was also thoroughly corrupt; among other offenses, he used municipal funds to deal in liquor and drugs. Vaudreuil's lax and crooked administration set an unfortunate precedent in New Orleans politics and reinforced the city's growing reputation as a place of low moral fiber.

The African Influence

The luxurious life of the wealthy Créoles was made possible by a regional economy based on slave labor. The first large shiploads of slaves arrived in Louisiana in 1719, and within five years the influx of Africans prompted the French government to draft the *Code Noir*, or Black Code. It mandated brutal punishments for slaves: Runaways could have their ears cut off and shoulders branded. The Code Noir also set up safeguards against cruel masters, including provisions that limited a slave's working hours and provided for adequate food and housing. The final article of the code granted to freed slaves "the same rights, privileges and immunities which are enjoyed by freeborn persons" and thus acknowledged a situation unique to Louisiana. Alone among North American cities it contained a large population of freed slaves, some purely of African descent, others of mixed European and African blood. The latter were known as *gens de couleur libre* (free persons of color), and they occupied a separate niche in Louisiana society. Each free person of color was assigned to a category based on his or her ratio of white

The Marquis de Vaudreil arrived to govern New Orleans in 1743, transforming the city into a hotbed of social activity and seamy politics.

A Créole couple poses for a photographer in the early 20th century.

to black ancestors. For example, someone with one black and one white parent was termed a "mulatto"; a person who was ⅞ black and ⅛ European was an "octoroon." The ratio system was so highly developed that the numbers even went into double-digit fractions. Today, the notion of a rigid caste system based on racial proportions is offensive and oppressive, but for Louisiana's gens de couleur the system offered certain benefits. They received more rights and enjoyed a higher status than they would have in the other slave-owning colonies. Outside Louisiana, all persons of mixed blood were lumped in with other blacks and treated accordingly.

The gens de couleur clung to their special status, identifying strongly with their French or Spanish heritage. Those who had a wealthy European father were sometimes sent abroad to be educated. The first anthology of black poetry in America, published in 1845, featured the work of a group of 17 free persons of color.

The gens de couleur were allowed to own property, and a small number of them even established plantations that, like the whites' holdings, were worked by slaves. Among this group of plantation owners was a determined woman named Marie Thérèze Coincoin. She banded with her children—the sons and daughters of a French planter named Claude Metoyer—to establish a prosperous, self-contained colony of gens de couleur libre in the Cane River country in central Louisiana. Many of her descendants became wealthy planters who sided with the slave-owning Confederacy during the Civil War.

Some women of the gens de couleur were groomed by ambitious mothers to become the mistresses of wealthy white men. At quadroon balls, beautiful mulatto girls were presented to Créole gentlemen, often young, unmarried men from good families whose parents thought this extramarital arrangement would school them in the ways of adult relationships. Once chosen as a mistress, a woman was set up in her own house. If she bore children, they were well taken care of and often educated in Europe. But the arrangement could end at a moment's notice if the young man found a "proper" bride. The mistress then kept her house and its furnishings. Offensive as this system was, it offered benefits that female slaves in colonial times rarely had: freedom and financial security. Some former mistresses became very wealthy women.

Louisiana's gens de couleur thrived until the 1860s. Ironically, Abraham Lincoln's Emancipation Proclamation, followed by the 13th amendment's abolition of slavery in 1865, brought about the group's decline. Once slavery ended, gens de couleur no longer received favored treatment. The situation worsened after the federal Reconstruction program—meant to improve the lot of southern blacks—failed and was abandoned in the 1880s. Thereafter gens de couleur, like other blacks, became victims of the discrimination that was rampant throughout the South. In the Cane River country, the descendants of Marie Thérèze Coincoin began to refer to themselves as "the forgotten people." Today, many blacks of French descent still live in southern Louisiana. They call themselves Créoles to signify that

In antebellum New Orleans, beautiful young women often were groomed to become mistresses for rich Créoles.

they, like the French and Spanish Créoles, have European blood.

The influence exerted by slaves and gens de couleur was powerful and lasting. Skilled black ironworkers created many of the delicately wrought iron balconies and fences that still lend the French Quarter its charm. Black chefs were responsible for originating Créole food, one of America's choicest cuisines, a delicious blend of local products prepared with French, African, and Caribbean techniques and seasonings. *Filé*, an herb of ground young sassafras leaves, was an ingredient used by the Indians; its presence in Créole cuisine—in dishes such as filé gumbo—reflects the Indian blood that numerous slaves also had.

The Spanish Period

Slaves imported from the Caribbean islands were auctioned near New Orleans's docks.

In 1764, King Louis XV—who had already ceded much of France's North American territory to the British under the Treaty of Paris—secretly deeded the remainder of his holdings, including Louisiana, to Spain, which

The large slave population was vital to the economy of Louisiana's sprawling plantations.

was ruled by Louis's cousin, King Charles III. The French government was relieved to be rid of the tropical headache of Louisiana, but when New Orleans's French-speaking colonists learned of the new arrangement, they lamented the separation.

In 1768, a group of French insurgents rose up against the new Spanish governor and forced him to flee to Havana, Cuba. The first colonial revolt against a European nation on American soil, its success was short-lived. Charles sent Don Alejandro O'Reilly, an Irish mercenary in the Spanish royal service, to suppress the rebellion. O'Reilly rounded up the leaders of the revolt. A trial was held and five of the rebel leaders were executed. Lesser conspirators received prison sentences.

Even before O'Reilly arrived, the revolutionary fervor was already waning. The French resented Spanish rule but got on well with the influx of Spanish colonials, and many of the prominent families intermarried. As before, French language and ways continued to dominate New Orleans.

During the Spanish period the population of Louisiana doubled. A prosperous sugar industry took root, and great plantations producing sugarcane, rice, tobacco, indigo (the plant that provides blue indigo dye), and cotton lined the banks of the Mississippi for 100 miles. The plantation owners depended heavily on slave labor. Of the nearly 43,000 people living in the territory in 1787, more than half were black slaves.

During this period two disastrous fires nearly destroyed New Orleans. Rebuilding began from the ground up; practically all the structures in the 90 square blocks that today make up the French Quarter were constructed when Spanish culture predominated. The simple, low buildings, built of brick, then plastered and whitewashed, conceal elegant interiors and charming private patios.

Despite the entrenched Spanish rule, several new groups of French-speaking immigrants arrived in America when the French Revolution of 1789 spurred thousands of aristocrats to flee the country. A number of them settled in New York and Philadelphia, but most were drawn to the South. They went to Charleston, where the French Huguenot influence remained strong, and to Louisiana, which was still regarded as French in spite of its formal allegiance to Spain. About 4,000 French are said to have come to New Orleans in 1791, including a troupe of actors, the first in Louisiana.

A second substantial wave of French-speaking emigres arrived after fleeing political upheaval in the Caribbean. In 1790–91, Santo Domingo (now the Dominican Republic) was the scene of two rebellions. The first was inspired by the French Revolution, which had resulted in the formation of a republican government. Taking their cue from this upheaval, a group of whites in Santo Domingo tried to start a revolutionary republican movement of their own. But they refused to grant basic rights to mulattoes and blacks, who then rose up against their white masters. The slave revolt quickly led to a massacre of the European population, and thousands escaped to the United States.

Both the Santo Domingan Créoles and the emigres fleeing revolutionary France often boasted aristocratic lineage. The wealthier among them brought along their possessions, including slaves, but others lost everything they owned and were forced to survive on whatever skills they commanded. Most gravitated toward the cit-

In 1764, Louis XV secretly deeded Louisiana to Spain, much to the chagrin of the region's French inhabitants.

With the signing of the Louisiana Purchase, the United States gained the territory that eventually composed part or all of 15 different states.

ies where French colonies, or at least a French heritage, existed; there the newcomers taught languages, dance, or music, or opened restaurants. If all else failed, they relied on the kindness of their fellow countrymen or courted American admirers of the aristocracy.

Santo Domingans continued to flock to Louisiana well into the 19th century, although their routes were sometimes indirect. In 1809, a group of refugees who had relocated in Spanish-held Cuba was exiled when war broke out between France and Spain. Nearly 8,000 former Santo Domingans, black and white, were loaded on American ships and sent to New Orleans, where they were reluctantly allowed to settle. Many members of this group were skilled tradesmen, easily able to earn their keep. They contributed an exotic Caribbean flavor to the cosmopolitan city.

The third major group of French speakers to arrive in Louisiana during the Spanish years were French Canadians who had also been thrust into exile. When, in the mid-18th century, the ruling British expelled them from Nova Scotia, the center of the former French province of Acadia, groups of Acadians settled along the bayous and on the lowlands of southwest Louisiana. There they evolved a way of life distinct from that of other French groups.

The Louisiana Purchase and Beyond

In 1800, a secret treaty ceded Louisiana back to France, now controlled by Emperor Napoleon Bonaparte. But Napoleon, prodigiously ambitious and bent on conquering all of Europe, needed ready cash. If he could obtain it by unloading his immense American holdings, so much the better: The Louisiana territory was more a nuisance than a help to his grandiose plans. U.S. president Thomas Jefferson sent representatives to negotiate a sum, and they were amazed when Napoleon agreed to sell the land for only $15 million—approximately four cents an acre. After signing the treaty of cession, Robert Livingston, one of the American negotiators, wrote, "This is the noblest work of our whole lives." The Louisiana Purchase was also one of the greatest real estate bargains in history.

Livingston's enthusiasm was not shared by the French in New Orleans. Once more they had been transferred to another foreign government. A colonial

New Orleans's wealthy Anglos built stylish mansions west of Canal Street.

Sugar and cotton plantations lined the banks of the Mississippi River until the Civil War.

official described their reaction as "stupefied and desolated. They speak only of selling out and going far away from this country." This grim response ultimately proved justified. Although the Créoles managed to hold on to their traditions and language for some years, despite the influx of the Americans, much of the Créole power and influence faded. They quickly lost their numerical advantage, and gradually their culture merged with that of the American mainstream.

Anglo-Americans poured into the huge new territory. (To get some idea of its size, consider that the

Louisiana Purchase eventually yielded the area of all or part of 15 different states.) A focus of American settlement was New Orleans, now the second largest port in the United States. Anglo plantation owners soon rivaled their Créole counterparts, and Anglo merchants brought an unprecedented shrewdness to New Orleans commerce. Few Anglos copied the example of Bernard de Marigny, a Créole planter who lost much of his family's enormous holdings through gambling, crop failures, and taxes. When he died at 83, having been reduced to living in a two-room apartment, de Marigny was heralded as "the last of the Créole aristocracy . . . one who knew how to dispose of a great fortune with contemptuous indifference."

The early 19th-century rivalry between the Créoles and the Anglos was reflected in the growth of New Orleans. Rich Anglos built stylish mansions west of Canal Street, the dividing line between the French and American sections of the city. These lavish homes were proof of the Anglo conviction that wealth ought to be flaunted, not hidden behind simple facades. Prosperous Créoles soon took the hint and established their own swanky neighborhood. In time, the proud Créoles accepted the presence of Americans and even intermarried with them.

During the War of 1812, when the young United States jousted with its former colonial master, the British army expected Louisiana's French residents to turn against the U.S. government. The British even distributed propaganda stating, "We make war only against Americans." To the Britons' surprise, the French remained loyal U.S. citizens. Even Jean Lafitte, a famous smuggler and rumored pirate, enlisted in the American cause in 1815. He and his men helped General Andrew Jackson win the Battle of New Orleans, the final conflict of the war.

Spiraling growth and new waves of European immigrants—including Irish, Italians, and Germans—figured importantly as New Orleans was transformed into a bustling metropolis. The city reached its peak as an economic and cultural center prior to the Civil War, when much of the mainstay crop of the South—"King Cotton"—passed through the port for shipment. The economic wealth generated a style of rich plantation living, but it declined in the wake of devastation wrought by the Civil War and by Reconstruction, the difficult period in which southern society was rebuilt and redefined. Yet New Orleans survived, surmounting

(continued on page 57)

In the early 1900's, New Orleans was still one of America's busiest ports.

CAJUN
COUNTRY

Most Louisiana Cajuns work close to nature. Some grow rice on marshy farms, others harvest maize with up-to-date combines, and still others fish the bayous that snake through the Mississippi Delta.

Cajun music originally featured unaccompanied vocals, but contemporary performers incorporate the accordion, the fiddle, and the drums in spirited arrangements that have won a nationwide audience.

Each February, Louisiana residents celebrate Mardi Gras, a bash that ushers in the sober fasting of Lent. Some towns hold informal cookouts; others, such as Church Point, stage an elaborate, full-dress parade the Sunday before the holiday begins.

Rural cajuns often gather to converse at the general store, such as this establishment owned by Otis Breaux in Leroy, Louisiana.

(continued from page 48)

floods and hurricanes and repeated epidemics of yellow fever, a deadly pestilence carried by mosquitoes that was not eliminated until the early 20th century.

Modern New Orleans is a vital seaport—the third largest in the world—and an international tourist attraction. Millions of tons of cargo pass through the port annually. Visitors stroll around the historic French Quarter and admire the mansions in the Garden District. They tap their feet to the sounds of jazz, invented in the city's brothels at the turn of the 20th century and now a New Orleans institution. New Orleans's cuisine is renowned worldwide. It is based on the finest traditional French cooking, accented with Spanish, Indian, and black influences, and blessed with a healthy helping of the local shrimp and crawfish.

But the city is best known for its annual late-winter carnival, Mardi Gras. A Catholic celebration practiced in Latin countries, Mardi Gras (literally, "Fat Tuesday") ushers in the somber fasting period of Lent. The festival includes parades of motorized floats mounted by elaborately decked-out "Krewe" members who toss trinkets and doubloons to thousands of shouting spectators, many of them tourists from all over America. New Orleanians in colorful garb hold "king cake" parties—if a plastic baby doll turns up in someone's piece of king cake (a plain bread dough cake), he or she hosts the next party. Mardi Gras attests to the undying tradition of Créole gaiety. *Laissez les bons temps rouler*— "let the good times roll"—remains the unofficial slogan of the residents of New Orleans.

Today, the French influence in Louisiana is reflected in a number of ways. The state's legal system is the only one in the United States based on the French Napoleonic Code (with some modifications from the Spanish era). Louisiana's 22 southern parishes (counties)—the "French Triangle"—are home to an estimated 1.5 million people, mainly Catholics, who claim French as a first or second language. Their influence

Populist Huey Long (at center, clowning with a vaudevillian) became a national figure during the depression, first as governor of Louisiana, then as U.S. senator.

has led to conflicts with northern Louisiana, which was settled by Scotch-Irish Protestants. Until recently, Louisianians in the northern parishes perceived themselves as having no influence in state politics, which was dominated by the more sophisticated southerners. In the 1930s, during the Great Depression, when thousands were unemployed, the champion of their resentment was a native son named Huey Long. Long, who improved the welfare and educational systems in the state, became the voice of all the "little people" of Louisiana, as well as the French Catholics, who helped elect him governor, then U.S. senator.

Throughout modern Louisiana, there is a resurgence of pride in the state's strong French heritage. In the early 1970s, a movement began to promote and preserve the French language. Like other Americans who have recently discovered their ethnic roots, the people of Louisiana are realizing that their cultural diversity is something worth celebrating. ∾

À LA FRANÇAIS

What do jeans, yogurt, pastries, and perfume all have in common? Nothing, except that they are often advertised as distinctively French as a means of expanding their appeal. The hometown bakery that promotes its croissants as "*à la français*" (made in the French style) is banking on the allure that French food has long held for people in the United States. Such advertising messages are merely proof of the deep attraction Americans feel for French culture.

The people who left France to settle permanently in America—a group ranging from political refugees and social visionaries to opportunity seekers—were responsible for part of the French influence in the United States. But other elements also played a role. An early friendship was forged between the two countries during the American Revolution and by the French church, which sent missionaries into the sparsely populated American wilderness.

Revolution and Friendship

The American Declaration of Independence, signed in 1776, aroused widespread admiration in France. Many French thinkers imagined the North American continent as a primitive wilderness where colonists and Indians alike lived in a "state of nature," uncorrupted by

When the English surrendered at Yorktown, the American forces were supported by the French fleet, which lay off the Atlantic coast.

power and worldly desires and infused with goodness and morality. Because of its noble-hearted populace and unspoiled environment, America would surely be the cradle of a new, superior civilization. Abbé Raynal, author of an influential work published a few years before the American Revolution, proclaimed that "[America], sprung from nothing, is impatient to take its place on the face of the globe and in the history of the world." When the American Revolution finally occurred, French money, troops, and ships proved crucial to the colonists' victory.

One reason the French supported the colonial rebels had less to do with the cause of freedom than with the relations between France and Britain. In 1763, the British had wrested away most of France's territory in the New World. The comte de Vergennes, King Louis XVI's minister for foreign affairs, reasoned that it was in France's best interests to support a revolt that would cost Britain dearly in terms of money and manpower whether or not the Americans won. In late 1776, Benjamin Franklin came to France to plead the Americans' cause. The affable, witty Franklin caused a sensation in Paris, and his deft diplomatic maneuvers, combined with news of the important American victory over the British at Saratoga, New York, in October 1777, persuaded Vergennes to press the king for aid to the fledgling nation. France formally recognized the United

States of America, and in February 1778, the two countries signed a treaty of alliance.

In the New World, news of the alliance could not have come at a better time: General George Washington and his men were fighting starvation during a desperate winter at Valley Forge. A French fleet dropped anchor at the mouth of the Delaware River in July 1778; a French expeditionary force landed in Boston in 1780. In 1781, a larger French naval force arrived in time for the famous march of French and American forces on Yorktown, Virginia. The ensuing battle ended with the surrender of British general Lord Cornwallis and his 8,000 men and effectively decided the war. With the struggle largely concluded, the French troops sailed home in 1782.

Many distinguished Frenchmen came to America to support the rebel cause, and they left a highly favorable impression. In Philadelphia and Boston, French officers

This plan of America's capital city was drawn up by French American Pierre L'Enfant in 1791.

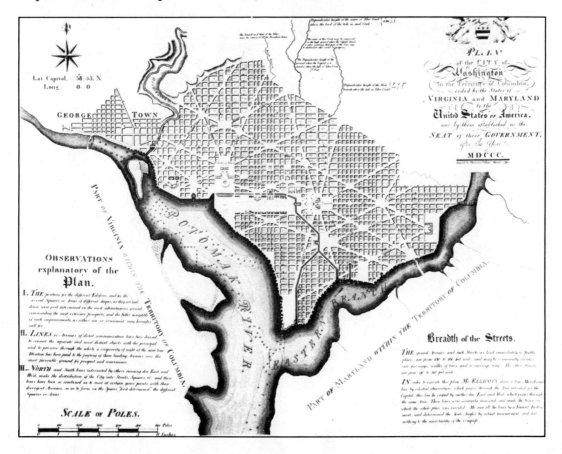

Alexis de Tocqueville's Democracy in America, *published in 1835, remains an invaluable analysis of life in the United States.*

were received in the best homes, honored at dinner parties and balls, and entertained with fireworks displays. The outstanding symbol of the French-American alliance was the marquis de Lafayette, who at the age of 20 was awarded the rank of major-general in the United States Army. To the Americans, the charming and passionate Lafayette represented the model Frenchman, an aristocrat who embraced the cause of freedom and human rights.

Even as the Americans were studying the French officers, so were the French scrutinizing their American hosts and hostesses. In letters and memoirs, the French recorded everything—including the Americans' fondness for drinking to each other's health, their astounding tallness, and their passion for French fashions and hairstyles. In subsequent times, France and the United States have been allies, yet their relationship has never again been quite so new or so enthusiastic as it was in the heady days of revolution.

French Travelers in America

One of the best studies of American democracy ever written was the work of a young Frenchman, Alexis de Tocqueville. In 1832, Tocqueville and a fellow official were sent to the United States to conduct a study of American prisons. The result of Tocqueville's nine-month visit was *Democracy in America*, published in 1835. This book and a companion volume brought out in 1840 analyzed the new democratic American society, and 150 years later Tocqueville's writings still have a wide audience.

A brilliantly observant traveler, Tocqueville stood out among a special breed of French visitors to the United States who studied the country and its people and described them in revealing letters and books. Michel Chevalier, who made an extended trip to the United States to examine its growing railroad system, sent home a fascinating series of letters that detailed the Americans' daily life. Writing in the 1830s, Chevalier and Tocqueville independently arrived at an interesting conclusion. Each predicted that one day the world would be split between two superpowers—the United States and Russia. Events of the 20th century have confirmed these travelers' foresight.

The Missionary Impulse

The Catholic church in France is an ancient institution, dating from the country's conversion to Christianity in the early Middle Ages. Just as the organized church left its mark on France, it helped shape French influence in the New World. In the early days of New France, Catholic missionaries made heroic efforts to convert the Indians. French-Canadian culture was shaped by the steadfast presence of the church; in the United States, French priests made up a significant part of the Roman Catholic clergy.

In 1789, only 25 Catholic priests lived in the United States, but after the French Revolution, the thousands of refugees who fled France included 100 Catholic clergymen. As the Catholic population of the country increased, missionaries came from France and Belgium to minister to the French-speaking Catholics spread throughout the vast expanse of the Northwest Territory and Louisiana, as well as to the French Canadians who had begun to move into New England.

The republic of Texas, which won its independence from Mexico in 1836, was also a focus of French missionary activity. Texas was predominantly Catholic as a result of its Spanish and Mexican inheritance, but Texans harbored ill feelings against Mexico, reducing the church's prestige. French missionaries diligently worked to revitalize Catholicism in the region, establishing convents, churches, schools, hospitals, and orphanages. Their efforts helped settle and civilize the Lone Star Republic, which joined the United States in 1845.

All of Texas was included in the diocese of Jean Odin, a missionary from Lyons, France, and the first bishop of Galveston. His travels in the 1840s were described with admiration by a journalist who accompained him: "Fearlessly and tirelessly he traverses the lonesome prairies on horseback, and through his restless energy and unassuming, charming personality has earned for himself the universal respect of those not of his faith."

In America such praise for a Catholic became rare in the 1830s and 1840s. An influx of thousands of Irish Catholics, fleeing famine in their country, sparked an antiforeign, anti-Catholic backlash among "native" Americans who considered themselves the true heirs of the nation's resources. The target of their animosity expanded to include other Catholics, who became objects of resentment, and mob violence flared up in places. In 1834, for example, the French Ursuline convent in Charlestown, Massachusetts, was torched.

Growing anti-Catholicism also affected the United States' perception of France. Long revered for its contributions to art, thought, and literature, the country now drew American suspicion. In the words of Howard Mumford, France was "the insidious foe, the seat of subtle propaganda and of a mysterious secret force." That force—the pope—was perceived as a power that dictated evil policies to the French Catholic nation.

American Francophiles

Not all Americans shared a suspicion of foreigners and Catholics. The nativist political parties of the 1840s—which sought to require 25 years' residence for citizenship—never managed to elect a president. Many Americans continued to admire French fashion, hairstyles, wine, and food.

One notable American who appreciated all aspects of French culture—books, art, and architecture, as well as luxury goods and rare vintages—was Thomas Jefferson. "Were I to proceed to tell you how much I enjoy their architecture, sculpture, painting, music," he wrote to a friend from Paris, "I should want words." Jefferson's lively interest in French architecture bore

fruit in his native state. His design of the Virginia state capitol (the first public building in the United States to be modeled on a Greek temple) was influenced by the French use of temple style. Jefferson also helped French architect Pierre l'Enfant plan the wide boulevards and parks of Washington, D.C.

In 1792 a French troupe performed the first opera presented in the United States. In 19th-century New Orleans, the manager of the lavish Théatre d'Orléans traveled each year to Paris to recruit the leading Parisian artists for his opera company.

By the 1830s, the influence of French fashion, or *mode*, was widespread in America. Frances Trollope, a British novelist who visited the United States, remarked on its peoples' slavish adherence to French fashion. Her book *Domestic Manners of the Americans*, written in 1832, notes sniffily that "the dress [in New York] is entirely French . . . on pain of being stigmatized as out of fashion." Wealthy New Yorkers who wanted the

French Americans built some of the country's finest Catholic cathedrals, such as St. Marie Church in Manchester, New Hampshire.

Virginia's State Capitol, designed by Thomas Jefferson, owes much to French architectural models.

most elegant and impressive furnishings for their mansions sent to Lyons for satin and velvet draperies, gilded mirrors, plush carpets, and marble and inlaid tables.

Among the rising middle and upper classes, a belief grew that a working knowledge of French manners and language marked a person as cultivated. In her novel *Little Women*, Louisa May Alcott gently poked fun at this vogue for things French. She shows young Amy March as more than a little proud of her command of the language, worrying whether a party she is anxious to give will truly be *comme il faut*—as it should be, or properly done.

When travel became a common leisure activity, Paris was a "must" stop on the tours of Europe made by wealthy Americans. Eventually, however, the taste for travel spread beyond the very rich. American artists and writers adopted the idea that a sojourn in France was essential for their artistic development. In the early 20th century, members of the "Lost Generation"—so dubbed by American writer Ernest Hemingway for the restlessness and disillusionment they felt in the wake of World War I—found inspiration overseas. Such literary giants as Gertrude Stein, Sherwood Anderson, F. Scott Fitzgerald, and Hemingway himself succumbed to the unending lure of Paris, the "city of light" that Hemingway so aptly described as "a moveable feast."

A Promised Land

Since World War I the French have not been prone to emigrate. Among the explanations for this, historians have cited the nearly flat growth rate of the French population—the French borders were not bursting at the seams with "huddled masses" eager to leave; France's relative prosperity, which made it a destination of choice among immigrants; and antiemigration pressure exerted on the French populace by the central government.

Some writers have proposed psychological reasons for the French reluctance to desert *la belle France*. In the view of American humorist Andy Rooney, the French have always been masters of finding happiness in their own backyards. Content with their lot, they are rarely tempted to seek a better life elsewhere. A slightly different version of this view holds that the French disapproved of the American way of life, which they saw as worshiping "progress," material goods, and modernization at any cost. Horrified by this society of callous strivers, the French stayed home. The truth of the matter probably touches on all of the above. The combination of a decent standard of living and a low population growth served to reinforce the traditional ties the French felt to their land and culture.

In earlier times, however, hundreds of thousands of French people did forsake their homeland for America, and for many reasons. The simplest, and most pressing, was a need to escape.

French fashions were the rage among sophisticated Americans in the mid-19th century.

Exiles

The first notable group of French political refugees was made up of aristocrats who fled the upheavals of the French Revolution of 1789. They settled in Philadelphia, New York, Charleston, and New Orleans. In 1815, after the fall of Napoleon Bonaparte, his supporters escaped the new regime to avoid prosecution. Many *Bonapartistes*, like the royalists of 25 years earlier, headed for the United States. Joseph Bonaparte, Napoleon's older brother and the former king of Naples, purchased a large estate in Pennsylvania. Another Bonaparte supporter, Achille Murat, became a successful planter in Tallahassee, Florida, where he wrote *The Moral and Political Sketch of the United States*, and struck up a friendship with American essayist and poet Ralph Waldo Emerson.

Separated from their hero by thousands of miles of ocean, the Bonapartistes refused to admit defeat. In 1818, a ragtag group of staunch loyalists—including veterans of Napoleon's armies as well as Spaniards, Americans, and several "reformed" pirates—established a colony on the lower Trinity River in south Texas. At Champ d'Asile (literally, "field of refuge"), they laid plans to rescue Napoleon from imprisonment on the Mediterranean island of Elba and then crown him emperor of Mexico. But the colonists, obsessed with military training, ignored the crops that were withering in the countryside, and imminent famine caused the collapse of Champ d'Asile. The settlers moved on to Galveston Island, headquarters for pirate Jean Lafitte, and from there struck out for Philadelphia or New Orleans. According to some accounts, Lafitte even lent them a ship.

The stormy politics of 19th-century France continued to account for periodic emigrations. Revolutions in 1830 and 1848, as well as the Paris Commune—a socialist uprising in 1871—drove new French dissidents to the United States. A final group of political refugees arrived after the fall of France in 1940 to Nazi Germany. This group of exiles included noted authors André Maurois and André Breton, painter Yves Tanguy, and artist Marcel Duchamp—who stayed to become a United States citizen.

Visionaries

A small number of French immigrants came to America for purely idealistic reasons. Buoyed by a vision of a better society, these people believed that a perfect—or

utopian—existence could be achieved in the untouched American wilderness. Unfortunately, these visionaries usually were city people ill-prepared for the rigors of the frontier. In 1848, Etienne Cabet led members of the Icarian Society of France to northern Texas, where he hoped to establish a completely democratic state in which each citizen would have the right to vote. In a little more than a year, however, many of the Icarians— who were mainly journalists and writers—perished of famine and disease. The remainder moved to Nauvoo, Illinois, to make a new start.

Texas was the site of another attempt at a utopian settlement. In the 1850s, the community of La Ré- union, established on 1,000 acres near Dallas, had 350 well-educated residents but very few practicing farm- ers. After a few years, La Réunion was dissolved, but its settlers were more fortunate than the hapless Icarians. A number of them went to Dallas, where they contributed to the city's business and cultural life.

Between Two Cultures

There were other scattered attempts to found French communities in the United States, but the majority of them failed. An exception was Castroville, a Texas town colonized mainly by people from the province of Alsace in northeastern France. The settlement bankrupted its founder, Henri Castro, but eventually it prospered.

Immigrant efforts at group living may have foundered because the French are a highly individualistic people. "Although the French understand organization as well as anyone," commented French historian André Siegfried, "they will cooperate only in an emergency." Thousands of French joined the California gold rush of 1849, but unlike the other miners, who preferred to work for companies, the French tended to work in private groups of four to six people.

After the Nazis occupied Paris in 1940, painter Marcel Duchamp immigrated to the United States.

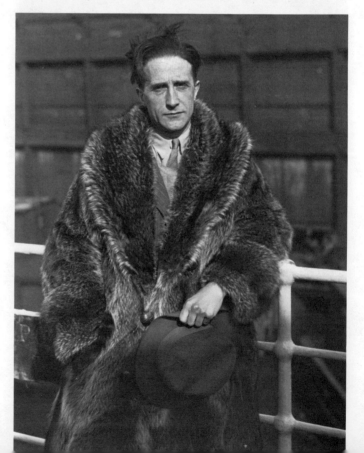

Arriving singly, for their own reasons, the French have succeeded or failed on their own merits. Quite often the French met with success because they came with marketable talents: Since the 18th century, many French immigrants have tended to be professionals—doctors, lawyers, and teachers—able to find ready employment. Even nonprofessionals usually have possessed some skill that was in demand. In the 1930s in New York, for instance, 3,000 French held jobs in the thriving restaurant business.

In general, the French immigrants who remained in the United States quickly merged into the social mainstream. During the boom years of European immigration, in the late 19th and early 20th centuries, large industrial cities such as New York and Chicago developed distinct ethnic neighborhoods—Italian, Irish, Polish, Jewish, and many more, composed of immigrant communities. But the French population in the United States did not adopt this pattern; there were few French enclaves with their own French bakeries, cafés, or schools.

It has been argued that the French immigrants blended in quickly because they were modernizers. Convinced that the United States was the land of the future, they willingly sacrificed their French identity in order to embrace American ways. Perhaps, too, they assimilated so easily because they were generally too few in number to band together in separate communities.

The struggle every immigrant has to face—clashes with American values, the invidious comparisons of the old and the new, the search for one's place in society—found expression in the remarks of Colette Montgomery, who emigrated from Paris to New York in 1946 as the 18–year-old bride of an American soldier: "It's not easy to be a newcomer to this country. You're between two cultures. You have to have a very strong identity to know who you are." Like all immigrants, the French experienced the hopes and fears that inevitably follow when people abandon a familiar land and become strangers in a new one. ❧

FOREST PRIMEVAL, FORESTS OF STEEPLES

This is the forest primeval. The murmuring pines and the hemlocks,
Bearded with moss, and in garments green,
indistinct in the twilight,
Stand like Druids of old . . .

These are the first lines of *Evangeline*, published in 1847. In this long narrative poem, American poet Henry Wadsworth Longfellow tells the tragic story of a doomed pair of Acadian lovers, Evangeline and Gabriel. Forced into exile from French Acadia, the two are separated. Evangeline begins years of difficult wandering to find Gabriel. When at last she reaches his side, there is time only for a brief kiss before Gabriel dies.

As drama, *Evangeline* is moving. As a description of the Acadians, it is idealized and misleading. The poem's popularity caused Americans to view the Acadians as a simple, rural people, a band of happy peasants, but in southern Louisiana, where many descendants of the original Acadians settled, the group had achieved quite another sort of reputation. The Cajuns, as they came to be called, resisted speaking English, preferring their unique brand of French. They were judged too fond of dancing and not fond enough of making money, and they considered formal education an unnecessary frill.

Certainly, the Cajuns are a more complex group than Longfellow depicted. They live primarily in two areas: northern Maine, which borders on the country from which they were exiled and has an estimated 200,000 Acadians; and Louisiana's French Triangle, which includes more than 800,000 people who claim Acadian descent. Cajun influence stretches into east Texas, coloring the "lapland" areas (where French Louisiana laps into Texas) of Beaumont, Port Arthur, and Orange, but the majority of southern Cajuns reside in Louisiana. A brief look through that state's local telephone books turns up columns of French surnames: Boudreaux, Fontenot, Landry, Theriot, Thiboudeaux.

In fact, most of Louisiana's French population is descended from the Acadians, not the European Créoles. The first Cajuns tended to have large families, and they easily absorbed other ethnic groups that settled near them. The Italians, Scotch-Irish, and Germans with whom they intermarried often adopted Cajun traditions, language, and music.

Originally, the Acadians came from rural areas of western France. In the early 17th century, they immigrated to New France and settled in the eastern coastal area known as Acadia and its neighboring regions, becoming farmers, fishers, hunters, and trappers. Large, close-knit families and communities helped ensure the Acadians' survival. Cut off from their mother country, living in a harsh, isolated land, the Acadians quickly developed a separate cultural identity; no longer French, they were not yet French Canadian. The Acadians' strong sense of kinship proved to be their salvation following 1713, when the Acadian homeland, long a pawn in the seesawing colonial wars between France and Britain, passed into British hands.

In 1755, Governor Charles Lawrence sought to end the threat of Acadian-inspired subversion against the ruling British. Lawrence had some grounds for suspecting the Acadians; although the Acadians officially were neutral in the conflict between Britain and France, they often sided with the French. Lawrence's remedy was to exile large groups of Acadians from the area, which had been renamed Nova Scotia, and open the area to British colonists. In 1755, about 6,000 out of a total of 15,000 Acadians were expelled in the first wave of a deportation program that lasted more than 10 years. Boatloads of Acadians were dumped in the 13 colonies (where, as Catholics, they were shunned), sent back to France, or packed off to the West Indies. Ever since, Lawrence has been portrayed as a pitiless tyrant responsible for causing unjust human suffering.

Despite tribulation and decades of wandering, the Acadians succeeded in retaining a sense of themselves as a distinct people. The first groups of Acadians filtered into southern Louisiana in 1765, and settlers continued to come until 1785, when 1,500 Acadians who had been making precarious livings in French port towns shipped into New Orleans.

Upon arriving in Louisiana, the Acadians settled north and west of New Orleans on the banks of the Mississippi, along Bayou Teche, and in the Lafourche Basin. Drawn to Louisiana because its population was, like themselves, mainly French and Catholic, the Acadians nevertheless chose to live in their own isolated communities. Describing their clannishness, a Spanish colonial governor characterized the Acadians as "a people who live as if they were a single family. . .; they give each other assistance. . . . as if they were all brothers."

Some historians believe that the Acadians avoided the French Créoles because they did not wish to submit to a class-ordered society. In any case a sharp line divided the two groups. Intermarriage between the Acadians and Créoles was rare; only the "genteel Acadians"—those who managed to accumulate some wealth—attempted to break into Créole or the equally rich and snobbish Anglo-American society.

In 1755, the British expelled 6,000 Acadians from Nova Scotia.

As a result of Louisiana's population explosion of the early 19th century, wealthy Anglos seeking plantations forced many Cajuns off their original land and onto swampy, marginal areas. As the Cajuns continued to move west, settling the grasslands of western Louisiana, their clannishness became more pronounced and their unique culture and folklore thrived.

Many 19th-century Cajun customs were based on a tradition of self-help. At the *coup de main* (lend a hand), neighbors gathered to cooperate on a large work project. The *ramassaerie* was a communal harvest, and at the *boucherie de campagne*, the hog-butchering for many families was done. The *veillée* was the hour at nightfall when the family gathered to talk, to finish light chores, and to sing.

Music played a large role in Cajun life. In the late 18th century, before instruments existed in the colony, the music consisted of unaccompanied singing. Then the violin arrived and dance bands were formed. At *bals de maison* (house parties), the distinctive droning fiddle and deliberately shrill voices of the singers accompanied the *contredanses* and *valses à deux temps*. Later on, the repertoire grew to include jigs, hoedowns, and Virginia reels, dances the Cajuns picked up from their Anglo-

Cajun culture includes homemade medicines, such as those being prepared here by Mrs. Louisianaise Daigle.

American neighbors. The Cajun bands came to be built around the fiddle and the accordion, an arrangement they borrowed from neighboring German settlers. Percussion was provided by washboard, triangle, or spoons.

Alongside the white Cajun music, an overlapping style was developing among black Créole musicians, the descendants of the gens de couleur libres. This style, called Zydeco, mixes Cajun, jazz, and rhythm-and-blues elements. Usually played at a faster tempo than Cajun music, Zydeco simplifies the melody and employs an accented—or syncopated—beat. According to legend, the name Zydeco (sometimes the variants Zodico or Zarico appear) comes from the first two words of the title of a dance tune, "Les Haricots Sont Pas Salées," ("The Snap Beans Aren't Salted"). (The missing salt is a reference to hard times.) The most famous Zydeco musician performing today is Clifton Chenier, who plays internationally with his Red Hot Louisiana Band. Recently, Cajun and black Créole music have both become popular, and many white musicians have begun to incorporate elements of Zydeco into their repertoire.

Contact with French-speaking blacks greatly influenced much of the Acadians' culture. The practice of voodoo (or *gris-gris*), based on a belief in the power of certain kinds of magic, can be traced to Afro-Caribbean roots. Despite a shared language and other common cultural traits, however, Acadians generally considered blacks a separate and inferior group.

"I Must Not Speak French on School Grounds"

Cajun group identity depends heavily on the language spoken by the community. At first Cajun French resembled the French spoken in the Acadians' land of origin, the rural areas of 17th-century western France, but a peppering of African, Indian, and Spanish words reflected the contacts the Acadians made in Louisiana. Although some English-derived expressions—for ex-

Twentieth-century progress has brought modern conveniences to Cajun homes, but it has not diluted their flavorful cuisine.

ample, *"back le char"* for "back up the car"—made their way into common speech, for years most Cajuns rejected learning English just as they shunned all formal education. Cajun parents were convinced that useful skills such as farming, fishing, trapping, and house-keeping—all taught in the home—constituted all the education their children needed. In the early 20th century, the illiteracy rates in the Cajun parishes in Louisiana were topped only by those in the predominantly black parishes, where the population was denied opportunities for schooling.

When Louisiana began enforcing minimum education laws, Cajun children were forced into the classroom. Even teachers who came from Cajun homes fervently upheld the prohibition against speaking French. Cajuns who attended schools during that time still have childhood memories of being made to write over and over, "I must not speak French on school grounds."

Despite this program, some Cajuns continued to favor their own language. Indeed, during World War II, Cajun soldiers in Paris found to their surprise that the supposedly "bad" French they were used to apologizing for at home was readily understandable to native French speakers. Sadly, though, the language spoken among blacks of French descent in Louisiana—a language related to Cajun French but with its own grammar system—seems to be disappearing even more rapidly than modern Cajun French.

The Perils of Progress

When a railroad line between New Orleans and Houston opened for business in 1880, the Cajun way of life quickly began to change. As the 20th century brought more technological advances, the distinctive Cajun culture seemed doomed to vanish altogether. Massive roadbuilding programs in the 1920s and 1930s ended the Cajuns' isolation in western Louisiana, but the old stereotypes lived on. Cajuns, scorned for speaking French, discouraged their children from using their native tongue. The mid-20th century oil boom in east Texas and Louisiana was a powerful economic magnet that drew many Cajuns away from their communities to work in the oil fields. As their earning power grew they purchased more modern goods, and an evening in front of the television replaced the veillée; refrigeration did away with the boucherie.

The Cajuns of the 1980s live like most modern Americans, regularly attending school and keeping abreast of national fashion trends. Recently, however, they have felt a resurgence of pride in their roots. As a result, Acadians in both Louisiana and Maine are making a determined effort to preserve their culture and language.

By 1900, Lewiston, Maine, had grown into a sizable "French town."

French Canadians: Strength and Enterprise

European immigration to the United States first occurred on a vast scale in the 1830s. The popular conception of the United States as a "melting-pot" of many different ethnic groups stems from that time, when millions of immigrants typically underwent tremendous hardships to make their way to the country they felt offered them the chance of a new life.

Among the groups immigrating to the United States were French Canadians from the province of Quebec, who actually began arriving in large numbers in the mid-18th century. Instead of crossing an ocean, though, the *Québecois* had merely to traverse the border dividing Canada from the United States. They settled in New York and in the upper midwestern states, including Michigan, Illinois, and Wisconsin, but their presence was strongest in the New England states. In the 19th and 20th centuries, cities such as Woonsocket, Rhode Island; Lewiston, Maine; and Manchester, New Hampshire, boasted sizable "French towns" that featured French bakeries, stores, banks, and French Catholic churches whose steeples soared above the neighborhood roofs. These *petits Canadas* (little Canadas) tended to spring up around the French Canadians' main source of employment in New England, the textile mills.

As late as 1905, when this photograph was taken, child laborers were a common sight in New England's textile mills.

This rare glimpse inside a mill worker's tenement dates from 1912.

As a group, French Canadians were not strangers to United States territory. Prior to the 1763 Treaty of Paris and the Louisiana Purchase of 1803, French-Canadian explorers, trappers, and settlers had canoed the network of northern U.S. rivers and the Great Lakes. Bienville, the founder of New Orleans, and his brother Iberville were born in New France. However, the most significant migration of French Canadians to the United States began in the 1830s, some 70 years after the British conquered Canada.

In the late 1830s, the French revolted against the British in Canada. When the British suppressed the rebellion, many French-Canadian leaders fled to northern New York and Vermont, and other discontented Québecois also crossed the border. Although this initial migration was not large (in 1840, the French-Canadian population in New England numbered about 8,000), it presaged the pattern of immigration the French Canadians would continue to follow. One of these early emigres published the first French-Canadian newspaper in New England, *Le Patriote Canadien*, thus establishing a long, proud tradition of French-language publications in the northeastern United States.

Throughout the 19th century and into the 20th, French-Canadian immigration continued. Unlike the Acadians, who were driven from their native land for political reasons, most French Canadians went south for economic gain. Because of sluggish industrial development in 19th-century Canada, French Canadians who came to Canada's cities from their small farms discovered that there were too few jobs to go around. To make matters worse, original farm holdings had been subdivided among generations of habitants, and with the acreage reduced to small plots of land that were tilled by farmers who used old-fashioned methods of cultivation, job prospects in the countryside were as bleak as those in the cities. This dearth of employment opportunities caused the Québecois to migrate to the booming textile mills of New England. They were recruited by mill owners, who were deprived of a convenient labor force as most native French Canadians and many New Englanders themselves streamed by the thousands to the vast, rich prairies of the Midwest.

Between 1860 and 1900, approximately 300,000 French Canadians immigrated to the United States. The exodus subsided in 1929; in that year the border was closed and the Great Depression began. Estimates of the total number of French-Canadian immigrants range from 750,000 to 1 million. The figures are vague because census records were imprecise and because many French Canadians considered themselves temporary residents. They crossed the border to earn money, but their cultural and historical ties remained in Quebec.

Unlike other immigrant groups, French Canadians were slow to become naturalized Americans; by 1940, only 56 percent of them had acquired citizenship. Among the reasons for this low rate was the French Canadians' desire to preserve their language, culture, and faith. They associated English with New England Protestants, and they were devout French-speaking Catholics. Unfortunately, their slowness in seeking U.S. citizenship cost French Canadians the right to vote, and with it the means of gaining political power.

Immigrants had an easier time finding jobs than they did achieving comfortable living conditions. In 19th-century Holyoke, Massachusetts, French-Canadian mill workers were crowded into dank, rat-infested tenements that contemporary observers described as "worse than the old slave quarters." Work was a family affair in which parents, children, and other relatives—as many as 10 or 12 from a single family—all labored. If the father was too old to tolerate the physical demands of the mills, he stayed at home cooking and cleaning while his wife and children went out to work their 12–hour shifts. A mill overseer once told a French-Canadian family that the law prohibited hiring children under 10 years of age. "The next day," the overseer recalled, "they were all ten." Like the Acadians, the Franco-Americans, as they came to be known, believed in putting their children to work at an early age and set little store by formal education because schooling did not further their immediate goal of survival.

The Bases of Franco-American Society

French-Canadian immigrants to the United States brought with them a traditional allegiance to the Catholic church. Parish priests, who normally exerted a great deal of influence over the daily lives of the immigrants, were French speakers brought in from Quebec, or if necessary, from France or Belgium. Priests stressed the value of education and helped establish parochial schools where lessons were given in French. Because the Catholic clergy disapproved of unions, French Canadians balked at joining the union movements gaining momentum in the 19th century. Indeed, they frequently were hired as "scabs"—or strikebreakers — thereby incurring the hostility of other workers.

Much of the French-Canadian separation from the mainstream culture was deliberate, stemming from a fervent wish to preserve their own language and religion. Especially in the mid-19th century, Catholics of all nationalities suffered fierce attacks from a group of bigoted native-born residents called the Know-Nothings. In addition, French Canadians found themselves struggling against the growing numbers of Irish Catholic immigrants over the issue of French-speaking priests. Branded with the derogatory name "Canucks"

Franco-American culture values large families and Old-World refinements.

and embroiled in clashes with Irish Catholics, Franco-Americans banded together to maintain their identity. In New England, particularly in the petits Canadas of mill towns such as Lewiston and Woonsocket, Franco-Americans rarely intermarried with other groups.

Franco-Americans also reinforced their culture by having large families. Into the 1940s, the parental bed was referred to as *"le manufacture de monde"* — "the people factory." Producing a large number of children aided survival because the bigger the family, the more potential workers it could field. At the same time, the family unit and the sense of French-Canadian identity it provided were both strengthened.

The traditions of the French-language press, begun with *Le Patriote Canadien*, endured for generations. More than 300 French-language journals, ranging from dailies to bimonthly editions, have been published in New England since 1839; their pages reported community news, ran installments from romance novels, and, most importantly, helped maintain French-Canadian ethnic identity. According to French-Canadian writer Jacques Ducharme, the papers of the 1940s carried appeals such as *"Parlez français á la porte de l'eglise et au sein de vos foyers"*: "Speak French outside the church and within your homes."

Even so, French-language periodicals had difficulty staying in the black, and many folded within a few months or years. Today, with fewer and fewer young Franco-Americans reading or speaking French, the periodicals have all but vanished.

Franco-Americans in the Eighties

Modern Franco-Americans no longer labor only in factories. They have moved beyond the "forest of steeples" that surrounded the old mills to become doctors, lawyers, teachers, and members of many other professions. And they have grown more active politically, making the effort to elect representatives of French-Canadian background to state and federal offices. Accompanying such progress, however, has been a decline in many Franco-American traditions. Few Franco-Americans speak French, and parish schools have eliminated their French programs. But like the Acadians, Franco-Americans are recognizing the value of their unique culture and are making attempts to preserve it.

The Marquis de Lafayette was one of George Washington's most trusted generals during the Revolutionary War.

PROMINENT AMERICANS OF FRENCH DESCENT

Over the past 450 years, Americans of French descent have excelled in dozens of fields, from educating the deaf to exploring wilderness territory. A roll call of important figures of French ancestry, and their achievements, would include people whose names were never heralded, yet whose actions made a difference: the industrious Huguenots, the brave *habitants*, the French-Canadian families who toiled in the textile mills. Given this range of achievement, the men and women profiled below ought to be seen as a sample selected from millions of possible candidates. Some still actively represent French culture; others, French in name only, have contributed to America as Americans. All of them have helped, in some way, to shape the modern United States.

Lafayette, the Hero of Two Worlds

From shore to shore, the United States has more than 40 towns and cities called Lafayette. Their existence bespeaks the great popularity of the French nobleman who became an ardent republican and loyal ally of the new United States. Gilbert du Motier, marquis de Lafayette, was 19 years old when he gave up active service in the French army. Leaving his wife and baby in

France, Lafayette sailed to the United States, determined to serve the cause of American independence.

When he arrived in the capital city, Philadelphia, in July 1777, Lafayette first faced the Continental Congress—a gathering of patriots and statesmen directing the revolutionary struggle. The skeptical congress viewed him as an adventurer bent on making a personal splash, but the young aristocrat's offer to enlist in the continental army without pay and his budding friendship with General George Washington cleared up this misconception. Lafayette joined Washington's staff as a volunteer, and by December 1777 was given full authority as a major-general of the Virginia light troops.

During the terrible winter of 1777–78 at Valley Forge, Lafayette shared the hardships of the American troops, earning the title "the soldier's friend." Lafayette fought with bravery and distinction and acted as a liaison between the American and French soldiers, smoothing the sometimes ruffled relations between the two allies.

Following the Battle of Yorktown in 1781, when American independence was assured, Lafayette wrote home exultantly, "The play is over, the fifth act is just ended." After the war's end Lafayette returned to France, where he continued to voice his support for a representative government. He actively aided the French Revolution of 1789, winning widespread popularity among the French people. By 1792, however, in the unpredictable twists and turns of the politics of the French Revolution, Lafayette's fortunes tumbled and he was forced to flee the country. In Flanders, Lafayette was caught by the Austrians, with whom France was at war, and he spent the next five years in foreign prisons.

Across the Atlantic, in the country he had helped liberate, Lafayette's star still glowed brightly. In 1803, in recognition of his contribution to the struggle for American independence, the U.S. Congress granted him 11,520 acres of land. Twenty years later, at the invitation of President James Monroe, Lafayette returned to the United States on a long, triumphal tour. Everywhere frenzied crowds greeted him with an outpouring of love and admiration. Lafayette did not live to see a republican government established in his native land. He died in 1834, after repudiating King Louis Philippe, a reactionary ruler whom he had helped gain power.

Although he has been styled the "Hero of Two Worlds" for his support of American and French republican movements, Lafayette has consistently received more favorable treatment in the United States than in France. Historian Albert Guérard, trying to account for French skepticism toward the man George Washington regarded as a son, observes that "Lafayette puzzles his biographers with his transparent singleness of mind and heart. Realists, in his own time and in ours, found it impossible to admit that a man could be so purely devoted to his principles."

Artist and Naturalist John James Audubon

The life of America's best-known naturalist is as compelling as any work of fiction. John James Audubon was born in 1785 on the Caribbean island of Hispaniola, the illegitimate child of a French planter and a local Créole woman. In 1789 his father took him to France, formally adopting him and providing for his education. In 1803, after studying drawing for a few months in Paris, Audubon traveled to America to live on an estate his enterprising father had bought outside Philadelphia.

In Pennsylvania, Audubon began his studies of American bird life. At this early stage, however, he was neither the passionate conservationist nor the rough-hewn pioneer his modern admirers like to depict. Audubon was an avid hunter, and garbed in the clothes of a Paris gentleman of fashion—satin pumps and silk breeches—he often roamed the countryside in search of game. After he had gone to France for a year's visit, Audubon returned to settle in Kentucky, where he tried various business ventures and pursued his interest in natural history.

John James Audubon adopted the guise of a backwoodsman when he made his firsthand investigations of American wildlife.

By 1820, Audubon had decided to devote his life to publishing his bird drawings. Supported by his wife, he went on expeditions across the country, including New Orleans, Niagara Falls, and the Great Lakes. His travels and studies resulted in the drawings that eventually were published as *Birds of America*. Publication of his masterwork began in 1827 with a large "folio" edition and continued over the course of 11 years. Audubon made several trips to London to oversee the engraving and coloring of his drawings and to sign up subscribers. As his fame as a naturalist spread, Audubon exchanged his silk breeches for country clothing and wore his hair long and shaggy, like a backwoodsman. Later expeditions led Audubon to Texas, Florida, and the coast of Labrador. He cowrote a text entitled the "Ornithological Biography" for the book *Birds* and began a series of animal drawings, which he was unable to complete before his death in 1851.

As a scientist, Audubon had limitations. Critics have pointed out that his beautifully drawn birds are at times caught in impossible poses. Yet the quality of his illustrations, prose, and observations of birds in the wild have brought joy to all who love nature, and they justify Audubon's lasting reputation.

This picture of a Louisiana heron was included in Audubon's masterpiece, Birds of America, *begun in 1827.*

John Frémont and the Adventuring Life

On October 19, 1841, John Frémont, a young surveyor, secretly wed Jessie Benton, the 17–year-old daughter of Missouri senator Thomas Hart Benton. Despite the powerful senator's initial opposition, the marriage turned out to be one of Frémont's wisest career moves and initiated a happy partnership. Throughout Frémont's career as explorer in the Oregon country, leader in California's fight for independence from Mexico, and presidential candidate, Jessie Benton Frémont served as an invaluable supporter, promoter, and ghostwriter.

Frémont was himself the product of an elopement between a French emigre schoolteacher and Mrs. Anna Pryor, who was unhappily married to an aged husband. Young Frémont was raised in towns throughout the South; after his father's death, the bright boy luckily found benefactors who underwrote his schooling. He joined the Navy, left it to become a surveyor, and honed his taste for exploration on an expedition with French scientist J. N. Nicollet to the plateau between the upper Missouri and Mississippi rivers.

After his marriage, Frémont embarked on several expeditions to the Oregon country. His detailed reports, cowritten by Jessie, of fertile soil and accessible trails to be found fueled the expansionist spirit of the times, and Americans poured into the Oregon country. In 1844, he made a daring winter crossing of the Sierra Nevadas in eastern California, and two years later, while leading an expedition to California, he suddenly found himself thrust into a leading role in the successful uprising against Mexico. He briefly served as civil governor of the new California territory, but ended his tenure at a court-martial in Washington, charged with mutiny and disobedience. During the trial public opinion heavily favored Frémont. When a guilty verdict was handed down, President James Polk commuted his punishment.

During the 1840s and 1850s, Frémont's restless energy led him to the Sierra foothills, where he worked a

General John Frémont commanded Union forces during the Civil War.

The Gallaudet Monument, erected in 1854, paid tribute to the founders of America's first institution of higher learning for the deaf.

gold mine; to a sojourn with his family in London and Paris; and to winter explorations of a southern railway route to the Pacific Ocean. In 1856, the national Republican party, hoping to capitalize on his popularity, footed him as a presidential candidate. Shy on funds and possessing little campaign skill, Frémont was defeated by James Buchanan.

In the initial stages of the Civil War, Frémont commanded Union forces in Missouri and western Virginia, but his military career was not a success. Then came a series of disappointments and failures, including a mismanaged railway scheme that caused him to be indicted in France. Frémont died in 1890 in California; his beloved Jessie outlived him by 12 years. Like Lafayette, Frémont is commemorated throughout the United States. From Idaho to Indiana, a score of towns, rivers, and peaks bear his name.

The Gallaudets

Modern society takes it for granted that deaf people are entitled to the same chances for education as people with normal hearing. In the United States, this equal opportunity is largely the achievement of a single family, the Gallaudets.

Thomas Hopkins Gallaudet, a descendant of French Huguenots, was born in Philadelphia in 1787. As a child he struck up a friendship with a deaf playmate, and he devoted the rest of his life to helping the deaf. Following studies abroad at the *Institut Royal des Sourds-Muets*, a pioneering teaching institution in Paris, Gallaudet returned to the United States, settling in Hartford, Connecticut. There, in 1817, he founded the first free American school for deaf children, the American Asylum. This institution marked the beginning of the Gallaudet family's dedication to teaching the deaf; Gallaudet's two sons, Edward and Thomas, devotedly carried on his work. In 1894, a school that Edward had founded in Washington, D.C., became Gallaudet College, the first advanced institution of higher learning for the deaf.

Kate Chopin and *The Awakening*

The United States has produced many authors of French descent, including essayist Henry David Thoreau, poet Henry Wadsworth Longfellow, and novelist Jack Kerouac (christened Jean-Louis Lebris de Kérouac by his French-Canadian parents). Despite their common ancestry, these diverse writers do not share a French outlook, nor do they in their works normally deal with French or French-American subjects. (Longfellow's poem *Evangeline* and Kerouac's *The Town and the City*, a novel based on his boyhood experiences in Lowell, Massachusetts, are exceptions.) Kate Chopin, however, was one writer of French ancestry who often relied on French settings. Her fiction depicts the culture and traditions of the Créoles and Cajuns she observed in Louisiana. Born in 1851 to a distinguished St. Louis family, young Kate learned French from her Créole grandmother. In 1870, she married Oscar Chopin, a Créole cotton trader from Louisiana, settling with him first in New Orleans, then on a plantation on the

Cane River. After her husband's death, Chopin took her six children back to St. Louis, where she began writing newspaper sketches about Louisiana. She gravitated toward fiction, and critics praised such tales as *Bayou Folk* and *A Night in Acadie* as charming illustrations of quaint French-American life.

In 1899, Chopin published a novel called *The Awakening*. It is set in the seductive atmosphere of New Orleans and the southern Louisiana summer resort called Grand Isle, where Edna Pontellier, the young wife of a New Orleans businessman, finds herself constricted by the narrowness of marriage and domesticity. Her "awakening" to the conviction that she must make her own way in the world and seek love on her own terms was a revolutionary theme for the time. The reviewers who had earlier praised her stories attacked *The Awak-*

Kate Chopin, shown here with her family in 1877, caused a sensation with her 1899 novel, The Awakening.

ening with such comments as "Not a healthy book" and "Leaves one sick of human nature." Disheartened by the critical and personal attacks that the novel aroused, Chopin wrote little else before her death in 1904.

Today, *The Awakening* is recognized as a major literary work. Chopin's reputation has been restored, and critics now praise Kate Chopin not only as a master of local color and a chronicler of picturesque customs but as a serious novelist with acute psychological insight.

Paul Prudhomme and the Triumph of Blackened Redfish

"When the taste changes with every bite and the last bite is as good as the first, that's Cajun!" writes Paul Prudhomme at the start of his best-selling cookbook, *Chef Paul Prudhomme's Louisiana Kitchen*. Prudhomme did not launch the Cajun revival, but he certainly has given many people the unique flavor of Cajun culture.

The youngest of 13 children, Prudhomme grew up on a sharecropper's farm outside Opelousas, Louisiana. After he became a chef, he traveled widely, working in many different places around the country, but the memory of his mother's Cajun meals brought him back to Louisiana, where in 1979, together with his wife, he

Houston's Dominique de Menil has amassed one of the largest private art collections in the world.

opened K-Paul's Louisiana Kitchen. This renowned New Orleans restaurant has lured many people to the Crescent City, and every night a long line is formed by patrons eager to sample Chef Prudhomme's okra or filé gumbos or his crawfish étoufee. This bisquelike soup, laced with pepper or Tabasco, contains garlic, the common New Orleans smoked sausage known as *andouilette* (pronounced en-DOO-ee), and generous amounts of crawfish. The demand for Prudhomme's highly seasoned blackened redfish (the fish is "blackened" by searing it in very hot oil) became so great that it threatened to destroy the Gulf Coast redfish supply.

Prudhomme draws a distinction between Créole and Cajun cooking. According to him, Créole cooking is a more sophisticated "city cooking," with a blend of ingredients from many cultures. By contrast, Cajun cooking, brought to Louisiana by the Acadians, has a simpler, heartier base influenced by country cooking. In most restaurants the distinction blurs between the two types. But Cajun or Créole, city cuisine or country fare, Chef Prudhomme's dishes inevitably draw delighted natives and tourists alike back for more.

Dominique de Menil: Dreams Come True

In 1987, the city of Houston, Texas, proudly welcomed a new major art museum. The formal dedication of the Menil Collection was a 40–year-old dream come true for Dominique de Menil, a passionate art collector and patron. Born in France, Dominique married John de Menil, a young baron from a military family, but instead of relaxing into the normal life of a rich French matron, she soon developed an interest in collecting and promoting the fine arts. The couple moved to the United States during World War II and settled in Houston, where they made enormous contributions to the growing city's cultural life, helping to transform the oil-based boomtown into a cosmopolitan center. At the same time, Dominique and John became involved in many social and humanitarian causes.

After her husband's death in 1973, Menil remained active both in social causes and in the art world. Her lifelong interest in art culminated in the opening of the Menil Collection, one of the largest private collections in the world. Housed in an elegant modern building, the museum, which offers free admission, contains more than 10,000 works ranging from African tribal sculptures to the creations of the Paris surrealists.

The humanitarian accomplishments of Dominique de Menil are no less significant. With former president Jimmy Carter, she has established an award series that recognizes people active in the worldwide struggle for human rights. The keynote speaker at the first annual ceremony was Bishop Desmond Tutu, a leading opponent of apartheid, the system of racial segregation practiced in South Africa. ❧

The Acadian revival includes the rising popularity of Zydeco, a unique form of music that mixes elements of many classically American sounds.

REVIVING THE LEGACY

More than 100 years ago, historian Francis Parkman commented on the epic struggle between France and Britain for control of North America:

> The most momentous and far-reaching question ever brought to issue on this continent was: Shall France remain here or shall she not?

Despite the bold coureurs de bois and the heroic missionaries, France lost the contest. The French legacy, however, remains; today, millions of people of French descent live in the United States and Canada. Parkman's query can well be applied to these people. Given the presence of so large a group of descendants, has France truly remained here?

In Canada, the answer must surely be affirmative. The 6 million French Canadians have kept their language and a sense of themselves as a separate group within the larger Canadian society. As a minority, the French speakers have been embroiled in numerous conflicts with the English-speaking majority. In the late 1960s, a separatist party emerged in the French-Canadian province of Quebec. The *Parti Québecois* advocated independence from the rest of Canada, by violent means if necessary. In the 1980s, Canada managed to reconcile the competing claims of its diverse citizenry. The Canadian government has addressed the desire of the French-speaking Canadians to preserve their heritage and bilingualism.

In the United States, the situation is more complicated. According to census figures from the 1980s, there are more than 14 million people of French descent in the United States. However, 11 million of them are not purely of French descent; in the "melting pot" that is America, it is not surprising that most report multiple ancestry. The majority do not speak a word of the language, nor consider themselves members of a separate ethnic group.

Of course, calling oneself an American does not necessarily mean ignoring one's ancient roots. Communities such as Castroville, Texas, and Vincennes, Indiana, which began as French settlements, preserved cottages and churches dating from the early 19th century. Descendants of the French Huguenots who fled to the original 13 colonies began to form Huguenot societies that still actively conduct historical and genealogical studies. All the same, Huguenot descendants, like most Americans of French ancestry, blended into the cultural mainstream. Those people who did not quickly melt into the dominant American society—the French in Louisiana and the French Canadians of New England— have provided the only surviving French cultural identity in the United States.

Cajun Spice: The Acadian Revival

Well into the 20th century, the term "Cajun" was an insult. To scold her child, a French Créole mother might say, *"Tu es habillé comme un cadien, ça c'est cadien."* ("You're dressed like a Cajun, that's Cajunstyle.") Beyond the bayous, Cajuns were scorned for their uninhibited enjoyment of dancing, music, cock fighting, and gambling. Their widespread illiteracy made them the butt of jokes and added to their isolation. Not surprisingly, the Cajuns returned the animosity; they held no high opinion of *les américains*.

In the early 1960s, in the face of social pressure, Cajuns began to modify their culture. French-speaking Cajuns, barred from better jobs, resolved to teach their children English and to stress the value of a college education. These changes resulted in a higher standard of living, but at the price of losing the old ways and Cajun French. The Cajuns seemed to accept the negative judgment others had made on their culture.

In the late 1960s and early 1970s, however, an abrupt reversal occurred as ethnic awareness soared throughout the United States. Cajuns displayed a new interest in their origins. Grass roots efforts to preserve and further the use of the French language culminated in the establishment of the Council for the Development of French in Louisiana (CODOFIL). CODOFIL placed an emphasis on developing standard or "proper" French rather than Cajun French. Instructors were brought in from Belgium, France, and Quebec to teach in the public schools. Cajun French speakers felt some resentment; their language was being brushed aside, once again, as somehow less acceptable, less real, than standard French.

The overall effect of CODOFIL to raise ethnic consciousness has been a positive one, however. In addition to administering language programs, the council sponsors festivals of Acadian music and crafts throughout southern Louisiana, whose 22 French parishes are now officially designated "Acadiana." Cajun French can be heard everywhere at these celebrations, which have become extremely popular among Cajuns and non-Cajuns alike. Young Acadians have discovered the charm of their ancestral music. Today it is played throughout southern Louisiana and Texas and featured on local radio programs, and it has attracted national attention.

Despite a similar stress on revitalizing the language, the Cajun revival differs in an essential way from the French separatist movement in Quebec. Cajuns express little bitterness toward the United States and have voiced no desire to break away from it. There is even a faction that, in true Cajun style, resists taking the

Bilingual newspapers such as Maine's Le F.A.R.O.G. Forum *seek to bind Anglo and French culture in the New World.*

In 1986 French president François Mitterand was the lone foreign dignitary invited to celebrate the 100th anniversary of the Statue of Liberty.

whole affair too seriously. This group heartily rejects the efforts of "genteel Acadians" to make their ethnic experience match Longfellow's prettified, pastel-colored story of Evangeline, and as "just plain" Cajuns, they prefer to have a rollicking good time.

There is even something of a national Cajun craze, especially among food lovers. Since New Orleans chef Paul Prudhomme caused a stir with his Cajun cooking, traditional and invented Cajun dishes have become standard fare on many menus. A potato chip manufacturer even brought out a "Cajun Spice" flavor.

Whether the taste for Cajun cooking will last in the American public does not especially matter. In the long run, it probably also does not matter whether enthusiastic scholars and folklore experts continue to descend on southern Louisiana in hopes of snaring interviews with authentic Cajuns. A sense of group pride has been awakened among Acadians that shows every sign of remaining vigorous.

The French Canadians: Toward Bilingualism

Like the Acadians, French Canadians in the United States suffered from the charges that their French was not "proper." Defenders retorted that their language differed in only minor ways from standard French and included expressions dating from the 18th century, when their ancestors arrived from France. Even so, self-conscious Franco-American children often avoided French-language parochial schools. After the 1930s, Franco-American writers began to notice an alarming decrease in French works. The experience of French Canadian soldiers in World War II, who were mocked by their fellow troops for their poor English, hastened the decline of French. By the 1960s, as intermarriage with other groups became common, French Canadians found that they were losing both their language and their cultural identity.

Faced with the prospect of a disappearing culture, Franco-Americans made determined efforts to uphold their spoken French. In 1960, French speakers in Maine—including both Franco-Americans and Acadians—won the repeal of a law that made English the sole language of instruction in the state's schools. Franco-Americans have encouraged the efforts of CODOFIL, and in 1978, French Canadians and French-speaking Louisianians held their first joint conference on bilingualism.

As part of the effort to support Franco-American culture, the New England/Atlantic Provinces/Quebec Center at the University of Maine has developed Franco-American study programs. Several New England states have sought to renew traditional ties with French Canada by signing cultural agreements with the Quebec government. Finally, like the Louisiana Acadians, French Canadians have begun to host ethnic festivals that promote their unique culture.

The nearness of Quebec has bolstered the Franco-American movement in the United States because many French Canadians are within easy reach of the Canadian land their ancestors left. Although Franco-Americans make the United States their home, they look to the north for their roots and maintain a strong pride in their heritage.

The Alliance Continues

On July 4, 1986, the United States celebrated the 100th anniversary of the Statue of Liberty. Millions flocked to New York City for the festivities, which included a week-long celebration that culminated in a spectacular blaze of fireworks. Had a Frenchman named Edouard de Laboulaye been alive to view the display over New York Harbor or to overhear President Reagan and French president François Mitterrand exchanging complimentary speeches at the relighting of Liberty's torch, he might well have nodded and smiled to himself. For it was Laboulaye who first conceived of the statue as a gift from the French people to America. In 1875, he expressed his wish that, in 100 years, the statue would "bear witness . . . to the everlasting friendship which joins France and America." Another Frenchman, Frédéric-Auguste Bartholdi, actually designed this majestic symbol of American freedom.

The French-American alliance, begun at the birth of the United States, has endured for more than 200 years, triumphing over occasional disagreements and several rough spots. During World Wars I and II, the United States paid back much of its debt for French support of the American Revolution when thousands of U.S. soldiers died on French soil, fighting to preserve that country's liberty.

In less dramatic ways, the two nations continue to maintain ties. American funds raised by such organizations as the Friends of Vieilles Maisons Françaises have been instrumental in the restoration of many of France's architectural treasures. The medieval ramparts encircling the small town of Provins, east of Paris, were rebuilt by monies donated by the American corporation IBM. In the United States, many large cities have a branch of the Alliance Française—French Alliance—which offers language courses and promotes cultural exchanges.

Few countries ever reach a perfect mutual understanding. If the brash American tourist lugging an oversized camera and speaking too loudly has become a stereotype among the French, so too have Americans created their own image of a "typical" Frenchman: a small mustachioed dandy wearing a beret, a lit cigarette dangling from one side of his mouth. Despite the stereotypes and the misunderstandings, France and the United States have shared a good deal of history and a common outlook. In a burst of enthusiasm, France's ambassador to the United States called the Statue of Liberty centennial celebration a "great day for French-American relations." For those Americans proud of their French heritage, there is a wish that the fine old alliance will continue for a very long time. ❧

FURTHER READING

Allen, Leslie. *Liberty: The Statue and the American Dream*. New York: Statue of Liberty—Ellis Island Foundation, Inc., 1985.

Ancelet, Barry Jean. *The Makers of Cajun Music*. Austin: University of Texas Press, 1984.

Bernier, Oliver. *Lafayette: Hero of Two Worlds*. New York: Dutton, 1983.

Ducharme, Jacques. *The Shadows of the Trees*. New York: Harper & Brothers, 1943.

Dufour, Charles L. *Ten Flags in the Wind: The Story of Louisiana*. New York: Harper & Row, 1967.

Hemingway, Ernest. *A Moveable Feast*. New York: Scribners, 1964.

McDermott, John Francis. *The French in the Mississippi Valley*. Urbana: University of Illinois Press, 1965.

Rushton, William Faulkner. *The Cajuns: From Acadia to Louisiana*. New York: Farrar, Straus & Giroux, 1979.

Stanforth, Deirdre. *Romantic New Orleans*. New York: Viking Press, 1977.

Zeldin, Theodore. *The French*. New York: Vintage Books/Random House, 1984.

INDEX

Picture Credits

POLLY MORRICE is a writer and editor. Her fiction, reviews, and essays have appeared in the *New Yorker*, the *New York Times Book Review*, *Cosmopolitan*, and other publications. She lives in Houston, Texas, where she maintains an abiding interest in all things French.

DANIEL PATRICK MOYNIHAN is the senior United States senator from New York. He is also the only person in American history to serve in the cabinets or subcabinets of four successive presidents—Kennedy, Johnson, Nixon, and Ford. Formerly a professor of government at Harvard University, he has written and edited many books, including *Beyond the Melting Pot, Ethnicity: Theory and Experience* (both with Nathan Glazer), *Loyalties,* and *Family and Nation.*